ENSLAVED

ENSLAVED

THE SUNKEN HISTORY OF THE TRANSATLANTIC SLAVE TRADE

SIMCHA JACOBOVICI & SEAN KINGSLEY

Preface by Brenda Jones

PEGASUS BOOKS

NEW YORK LONDON

ENSLAVED

Pegasus Books, Ltd.
148 West 37th Street, 13th Floor
New York, NY 10018

First Pegasus Books cloth edition October 2022
First Pegasus Books paperback edition May 2023

Interior design by Maria Fernandez

Library of Congress Cataloging-in-Publication Data is available.

ISBN: 978-1-63936-458-9

10 9 8 7 6 5 4 3 2 1

Printed in the United States of America
Distributed by Simon & Schuster
www.pegasusbooks.com

Dedicated to all those, past and present, who have been enslaved.

CONTENTS

PREFACE

by Brenda Jones

The descendants of enslaved peoples represent an inconvenient truth. Conceived in a boiling cauldron of naked ambition and insatiable greed, we are the progeny of a false belief that the vestiges of untold violence, theft, human degradation, and exploitation can somehow escape their unholy origin and launch into a kind of buoyant forgetfulness. This imagined culmination of all the darkness that came before is a wishful, radiant resolution, a voyage into light to a place where every crime is not only forgotten, but somehow erased. The perpetrator is left clean, pure, and fully absolved, regardless of the heaving damage of the original sin.

After all, who could not justify what any creature believes it must commit within the primeval struggle to survive? Existence is paramount above all other values, wouldn't you agree? So, if some threats require the momentary sacrifice of the soul, the choice is swift and overwhelmingly justified. The soul has an infinity of eons to purge any trace of violation and return finally to oneness with the light.

Maybe had you or I felt the gnawing anxiety of that hunger scratching for relief or the humiliated nakedness of a poverty so persistent it birthed a bitter identity . . . maybe if we knew firsthand the generations of longing to be bathed in riches, and maybe if we had barely survived the freezing darkness through ages of deprivation, perhaps we would sympathize with the furious demand of this greed. Perhaps . . . But if we have learned anything over the course of these last six centuries, maybe, just maybe, we now comprehend that what is eternal can never, ever be erased.

We can delay and evade its insurgency, seem to temporarily impede its appearance, but what was meant to be can never be eradicated, even by atomic force. Life can never be completely stamped out. Its remnants will reconstitute if a will beyond our own was its Creator.

Even a valley of dry bones can still be uncovered, unearthed, and scraped together to convey the most salient, present-day truths. Of course, all the gorgeous details are lost—the locks of sumptuous, thick hair, the interesting curl of the lips that runs in the family, those deep-set, penetrating eyes passed down through generations. And the tender details of each individual story are gone too—all the secrets forged in terror, the recollections of amazing grace extended by the Spirit even in the most dire circumstances, the trauma of capture and its impact will never be precisely known or submitted to a lineage of protection passed down by the tribal griot from generation to generation.

Every treasure more than twelve million people were birthed and blessed to convey has been lost. There are spaces in time—lapses—silence across generations of uncertainty. There is so much we will never know, but what we need to know, the essence of the lesson their lives were meant to teach, remains there. It is still available, found in evidence, strewn across the ocean floor waiting to be reconstructed and remembered to share its unvarnished treatise on the human condition.

The descendant's existence conveys the disturbing reminder that there is no "place" to hide as long as the soul remembers even a tinge of its violent origin. Somehow the truth of that inception is always borne out. Our origin can never be erased. You might believe the miseducation, indoctrination, institutionalization, acceptance, wealth, fame, or a subsistent life led in abject obscurity would minimize any trace of memory to its tiniest insignificance. But the truth is the more you have, the more readily you realize that having does not satisfy. The more you have, the more clearly you hear the call of the inner life.

The more you know, the more you realize that forgetting is an illusion. It is remembering that is freeing. References to the Middle Passage resonate throughout African diaspora literature and art. What cannot be recounted by experience is reimagined, repurposed, visited by the mind again and again.

It is remembered in Paule Marshall's *Praisesong for the Widow* and Toni Morrison's Nobel Prize-winning masterpiece *Beloved*. It is the backdrop of Charles Johnson's National Book Award-winning novel *Middle Passage*, the fictional story of a fateful voyage on a slave ship, and also the foundation of V. S. Naipaul's Trinidadian classic by the same name. The great playwright August Wilson begins his tour de force ten-play cycle capturing each decade of the twentieth century with *Gem of the Ocean*, involving a psychic voyage to the bottom of the ocean floor to a great city of bones occupied by the spirits of our ancestors who leapt to their death or were killed and spared the sacrilegious indignities ahead.

In the verse of "Slave Driver," Bob Marley remembers a turmoil he never experienced, and his rage is fresh as though it happened only weeks before. Even a modern-day bard, Jay-Z, speaks of the anomaly in his "Oceans" rap. He muses on the irony of his wealth juxtaposed with the tragic origins of his ancestors. He depicts himself in a tuxedo, riding in a fine car and still remembering what the soul can never release. It has never been forgotten, no, not even by those who know only that it happened and nothing else. Forgetting is an illusion but remembering is well on the path to liberation.

The descendants of enslaved peoples represent all of this inconvenient truth. We are born in innocence, but we learn quickly that we are the living, breathing embodiment of a harvest of crime and centuries of violation others wish they could forget. Our existence is a reminder of an indelible inception, but it also conveys an abiding hope. We mean a mistaken past can indeed lead to a promising future. Yes, we are the living evidence that "truth pressed to earth will rise again," that "you can kill a human being," as activists and revolutionaries say to ward off the terminal potential consequences of protest, "but you cannot kill the idea that person represents."

Secretly, even to the perpetrator caged by his or her knowledge of unforgivable sin, it is a relief to know that, despite the darkest of intentions and the horror of the crime, there is a divine spark that can never be erased. Only so much damage can ever be done. If only they knew our survival is a dynamic part of the offender's dream of salvation. Our existence teaches, the one powerful lesson all war and violence ultimately convey. That truth applied to human existence has the capacity to quench the insatiable hunger and bring an end to shame forever.

The words have been spoken since the beginning of time by poets, sages, and philosophers. Lately a moral leader, Rep. John Lewis, said it best; "We are one people," he would preach, "one family, the human family. And we all live in one house, the American house, the world house. We must learn to live together as brothers and sisters or we will all perish together as fools." He would say, "every human being is a spark of the divine," and once we become deeply aware of the sanctity of all life, we will be destined to build what he called "a Beloved Community, a nation and a world society at peace with itself."

Just imagine what would happen if we finally decided to learn from millennia of mistaken violence; the freedom we are all seeking would not be far behind. Who knew that the conservation law of energy we studied in high school science class had philosophical, historical, and even moral implications? Energy is never destroyed. It is only transmitted, transmuted, and transformed. And this is why to this day, hundreds of years later, this book and the *Enslaved* series that it grew out of can teach. The flesh is gone, but the bones of the lesson are still with us. The more we remember, the more we can heal, and the more we know what happened and how it happened, the more we can transform our future.

—Brenda Jones
Washington, DC

INTRODUCTION

O ver four hundred years, twelve million Africans were trafficked to the "New World". The largest forced migration in history. Almost two million died en route.

Portuguese, British, French, Spanish, Dutch, Danish, and American traffickers branded Africans like cattle, cut off their hair, raped women in forts like Elmina in Ghana, and, as the Capuchin priest Dionigi de Carli put it in 1667, herded Africans into ships' holds where they were "press'd together like Herrings in a Barrel . . ."

On the Atlantic waves, male captives were locked in chains. Rebels who refused to eat had their mouths forced open with iron vices or were killed and hanged on masts as warnings to the others. When they were sold onto plantations in the Caribbean and Americas, the names of the trafficked millions were changed to Christian ones. The stripping of a continent's human identity was complete.

At the epicenter of this enforced exodus was the ocean and the ships. Until recently, the technology to find lost and forgotten slave wrecks had been limited. The hatches of sunken history stayed bolted. Now, mixed gas diving, using rebreathers, lets humans descend beyond one hundred meters. Remotely and Autonomously Operated Vehicles (ROVs) extend the limits of exploration beyond four thousand meters in depth.

Taking advantage of these new technologies, over a period of two years from 2017 to 2019, a group of divers from the Florida-based Diving With A Purpose (DWP), an organization affiliated with the National Association of Black Scuba Divers (NABS), dived seven sunken slave ships and two sunken "feedom boats." No one had ever dived so many sunken slave ships. No one had ever dived a sunken freedom boat, confirmed to have spirited runaways from the American South to freedom in Canada.

In this exploration, the divers sought to give voice to the forgotten millions whose memories were drowned by Western greed and profit. They also wanted their discoveries to be springboards inspiring deeper investigations into the transatlantic slave trade.

At the center of the trade was sugar. Prices were kept low by a system of slavery that was meticulously planned at every stage and touched every corner of the globe. The trade *was* driven by sugar, but also by coffee, chocolate, and tea, all highly addictive. The world was hooked. The London bookshop owner William Fox, who opposed the slave trade, warned Britain in 1791 that every spoonful of West Indian sugar taken in tea and coffee was mixed with the blood of Africans. In 1870s England, an aging former African slave called Caesar remembered the evil days of sugar production. He explained how, after wearing his slave chains for decades, "the iron entered into our souls!"

Enslaved is the first book to tell the story of the transatlantic slave trade from the bottom of the sea, but it is far from just a story of victims. Enchained Africans did not accept their fate without a fight. One in ten slaving voyages ended in revolt. Reflecting this reality, ours is also a tale of heroes—resistance, revolution, and the survival of African culture in the face of unimaginable odds.

Diving With A Purpose's efforts were captured in the six-part series *Enslaved: The Lost History of the Transatlantic Slave Trade* that featured Hollywood icon Samuel L. Jackson and has now led to the book you are holding. Writing the book allowed us to dive deeper into the history. It's been an incredible journey. Shipwrecks and marine archaeology are a uniquely tangible way of encountering the past.

For divers Kramer Wimberley, Alannah Vellacott, Kinga Philipps, and Joshua Williams, theirs was also a voyage of self-discovery. They are a very special group of people united by a desire to seek out the truth and to do so fearlessly.

This is their story.

—Simcha Jacobovici & Sean Kingsley,
Tel Aviv & Virginia Water

FOLLOW THE MONEY

It has been said, Will you, for the sake of drinking rum, and sweetening your coffee with sugar, persevere in the most unjust and execrable barbarity?

—Captain John Stedman, *Narrative of a Five Years Expedition Against the Revolted Negroes of Surinam*

(1796)

BAD IDEAS

Fort Zeelandia—Paramaribo, Suriname

The transatlantic slave trade would never have happened if it did not generate money. Tons of money. Much of the world we live in today was built on the back of enslaved Africans. Or as the author of *Robinson Crusoe*, Daniel Defoe, put it so crudely in 1713, "No African Trade, no Negroes, no Negroes, no sugar; no Sugar, no Islands, no Islands, no Continent, no Continent, no Trade." Modern historians go even further: no slave trade, no Industrial Revolution, and no Western civilization as we know it.

To find out how such vast machinery—bad ideas, ships, sugar, and coffee factories—made the world smaller, connecting superpowers and capital cities to the most remote parts of Africa, the Caribbean, and Latin America, you need to follow the money.

The bigger the rewards, the greater risks were taken in the worship of profit. Wrecked ships were sometimes the result of this human greed. Even when their trafficked human cargos ended up sunk in some ghastly outpost of empire, Europe still found appallingly innovative ways to win. In Holland and England, you could insure enslaved Africans sunk at sea and still cash in your policy. Sink or sell was a win-win result for heartless traders.

Today, a crack group of intrepid divers, marine archaeologists, dirt archaeologists, historians, and experts in ocean technology, inspired and challenged by the activist and Hollywood legend Samuel L. Jackson and his wife LaTanya Richardson Jackson, are bringing the forgotten back to life. The responsibility falls on the shoulders of a group of Americans: Diving With A Purpose (DWP), which wants answers and action to make sense of centuries of suffering. They plan to dive for truth on a series of slave wrecks and put history on trial. Most of their former exploration has focused on America. Their facemasks, fins, and wetsuits are packed to travel the globe and hunt down the seas' great sunken ships to lay bare these forgotten tragedies.

To come to grips with the demons of the colonial past, Diving With A Purpose's haunting journey will take them to four continents and nine shipwrecks that change the perspective and conversation. Rather than just read what English sea captains wrote and conveniently left out of the pages of history, they want to physically touch and reconstruct the forensic archaeology.

The team seeks justice so the souls of their ancestors can finally rest. This is a personal journey about origins and roots. Above all, this time traveling is giving voice to the silence, breathing new life into people of color still living with unanswered questions. For the first time, the team is telling the history of the transatlantic slave trade from the bottom of the ocean.

DIVING WITH A PURPOSE

Diving With A Purpose (DWP), based in Biscayne National Park, Florida, specializes in education, training, certification, and field experience in maritime archaeology and ocean conservation. DWP's goals are to protect, document, and interpret African slave trade shipwrecks and the maritime history and culture of African Americans worldwide. Its divers learn how to use archaeological remains to tell stories that are not in the history books.

Since 2005, DWP has trained 350 adults and a hundred children. Its divers work on slave ships, World War II plane crash sites, and have joined expeditions with the National Oceanic Atmospheric

Administration (NOAA). DWP is a global partner in the Slave Wrecks Project in collaboration with the Smithsonian's National Museum of African American History and Culture, George Washington University, Iziko Museums of South Africa, and the US National Park Service.

Teams from DWP have partnered in the recovery of the *São José*, a Portuguese slave vessel lost off Cape Town in 1794 on its way from Mozambique to Brazil. Of the 512 African captives onboard, 212 died. DWP was part of the discovery of the *Clotilda* in the Mobile River off Alabama, the last known slave ship to arrive in the United States, fifty-two years after the traffic in enslaved Africans was legally abolished.

Alannah Vellacott, Kramer Wimberley, and Kinga Philipps had crossed the Atlantic to Suriname to listen to a story they did not want to hear. And then to dive a haunted slave wreck they did not want to dive. There was no option. The sinking of the Dutch West India Company trader the *Leusden* in the Maroni River on January 1, 1738, witnessed the single largest human tragedy in the history of the transatlantic slave trade. Diving With A Purpose had flown in their gear to shine a spotlight on one of the most horrific crimes of the transatlantic slave trade, forgotten by the world for three hundred years.

Paramaribo, the capital and leading port city of Suriname, was a Dutch slave colony 350 years ago, colonized with one purpose in mind: to enrich the Netherlands. Built on a perilous reef, its waters choked by rolling sandbars that made navigation hazardous, fertile lands fed by mighty rivers swept far inland. Artificial Dutch canals cut deep into Suriname's rainforests made communications excellent and Paramaribo choice real estate for the grinding cogs of sugar and coffee growing.

The town was a land of order, if not law. Straight streets were lined with orange, tamarind, and lemon trees in what seemed like everlasting bloom. Two- to three-story houses—1,400 by the late eighteenth century—were built of fine timber and brick foundations. At night the Dutch slept in cotton hammocks in rooms stacked with crystal chandeliers, paintings, and china jars.

Life was good. As Captain John Stedman put it in his *Narrative, of a Five Years' Expedition Against the Revolted Negroes of Surinam* in 1796, in Paramaribo, "The town appeared uncommonly neat and pleasing, the shipping extremely beautiful, the adjacent woods adorned with the most luxuriant verdure, the air perfumed with the most utmost fragrance, and the whole scene gilded by the rays of an unclouded sun."

The dive team walked through a forbidding stone archway shrouded in darkness and emerged from the shadows into the courtyard of Fort Zeelandia. Back in the day, the fort was the most striking building in Suriname. Built to store and sell newly landed African captives and goods for export, its prospect looked far more hospitable than the stone prison-castles studded along West Africa's Gold Coast. Four Dutch-style mini manor houses opened onto a large square, its paving made from red tiles set sideways, imitating the streets of Amsterdam. At its center, a tiled floor and stone sundial formed a welcome sanctuary to impress the world about the Netherlands' powerful reach across the waves.

Fort Zeelandia, built by the French in 1640, was this shore's latest incarnation. Lord Francis Willoughby planted an English flag over the Indian village of Torarica in 1651 and, in an act of smug self-glorification, renamed it Willoughbyland. Soon the town bustled with three thousand enslaved Africans and a thousand European settlers. The Dutch repaid the invasion courtesy in 1667 when they swapped control of Nova Zeelandia with the British, at the end of the Second Anglo-Dutch War, in exchange for a swamp they owned elsewhere in the New World that they thought would come to nothing. It was called New Amsterdam, now New York City. As Suriname's new masters put it, by their smart dealing the Dutch "taught the covetous Britons good manners."

The lords from the lowlands ruled over 175 mixed plantations. In the country with no winter, they found paradise. Small deer, stags, and butterflies frolicked across the countryside. In the town, Dutch merchants and plantation masters amused themselves feasting, dancing, riding, playing cards, and visiting their small theater. By the end of the eighteenth century, the colony's five thousand Europeans had seventy-five thousand slaves to attend to their every need.

COLONIAL DUTCH PARAMARIBO

From Captain J. G. Stedman, *Narrative, of a Five Years' Expedition, Against the Revolted Negroes of Surinam, in Guiana . . . from the Year 1772, to 1777 . . . Volume I* (London, 1796).

"The town of Paramaribo has a noble road for shipping, the river before the town being above a mile in breadth, and containing sometimes above one hundred vessels of burthen, moored within a pistol shot of the shore; there are indeed seldom fewer there than fourscore ships loading coffee, sugar, cacao, cotton, and indigo, for Holland, including also the Guinea-men that bring slaves from Africa, and the North American and Leeward Island vessels, which bring flour, beef, pork, spirits, herrings, and mackarel salted, spermaceti-candles, horses, and lumber, for which they receive chiefly melases to be distilled into rum . . ."

"Paramaribo is a very lively place, the streets being generally crouded with planters, sailors, soldiers, Jews, Indians, and Negroes, while the river is covered with canoes, barges, &c. constantly passing and repassing, like the wherries on the Thames, often accompanied with bands of music; the shipping also in the road adorned with their different flags, guns firing, &c.; not to mention the many groupes of boys and girls playing in the water, altogether form a pleasing appearance . . . Their carriages and dress are truly magnificent; silk embroidery, Genoa velvets, diamonds, gold and silver lace, being daily worn, and even the masters of trading ships appear with buttons and buckles of solid gold. They are equally expensive at their tables, where every thing that can be called delicate is produced at any price, and served up in plate and china of the newest fashion, and most exquisite workmanship. But nothing displays the luxury of the inhabitants of Surinam, more than the number of slaves by whom they are attended, often twenty or thirty in one family."

Fort Zeelandia's twenty-one cannons sticking out from two forti-fied bastions, commanded everything coming in and out of the Atlantic Ocean, fifteen kilometers away, and the Suriname River. Nothing got by without the commander tipping his hat. In one sweep from its riverbank, the eye takes in a panorama of power and profit where slaves arrived and sugar was sent downstream and on to Europe. The muddy gray waters saturated with dank forest soils looked less like home in the Florida Keys and even murkier than the English Channel. Alannah, Kramer, and Kinga were in for a tough mission.

Today most of old Zeelendia is gone. Paramaribo is sliced up by concrete bridges spanning the Suriname River. Juggernauts of the sea slowly haul goods across the water. Most of the city's money comes from bauxite, the main ore used to make aluminum. Downtown, the gold-painted wooden beams of the old Dutch Saint Peter and Paul Basilica and the De Waag, Weighing House, where agricultural goods were sorted for shipment, still stand.

In Fort Zeelandia's central courtyard, Alannah, Kramer, and Kinga had arranged to meet Dr. Leo Balai from the University of Amsterdam. Dr. Balai is a man on a mission who badly needed the dive team's help.

"I want to tell you a story I think nobody wanted to tell," he began. "A story I need to tell because it's so important. It's a story about the biggest mass murder in the history of the transatlantic slave trade. It's the story of the *Leusden*."

Unlike most slave ships, the *Leusden* was one of the very few Dutch ships built specially for the slave trade. Its last voyage began in Ghana on November 19, 1737. The crew enjoyed a smooth trip, taking just forty-four days to cross the Middle Passage linking West Africa and South America. Then, on December 30, everything went wrong. It started to rain; a dense fog fell. Eventually one of the sailors, desperate for relief, shouted, "Land ahoy!" Crew and captain thought they had reached the mouth of the Suriname River and the safety of journey's end. They were about to make a fatal mistake. They had taken a wrong turn, swinging inland ninety-five kilometers too early into the Maroni River.

THE *LEUSDEN*

- One of last slave ships of Dutch West India Company
- 33.9 meters long, 9.0 meters wide, 3.6 meters deep
- 10 slave voyages, 1719 to 1738
- 6,564 captives embarked, 1,639 died at sea
- Left Elmina in Ghana, November 19, 1737, with 700 African captives, for Suriname
- Wrecked, January 1, 1738, mouth of the Maroni River, Suriname
- The crew bolted closed the hatches; 664 Africans were left to drown
- 23 kilograms of gold for Amsterdam was recovered

THE DUTCH SLAVE TRADE

The earliest Dutch trading voyage to West Africa was made in 1593 by Barent Ericksz. Over the years the Dutch transported nearly 500,000 captives out of West Africa, about 5 percent of Europe's total. During the 175 years of their involvement, their share of the trade approached 10 percent of all traffic, however. For short periods in the 1630s and 1640s, the Dutch were dominant.

Between 1730 and 1791, the West India Company and Dutch free traders combined trafficked 268,792 Africans in 906 ships: on average 1,500 captives a year between 1630 and 1674, 3,000 up to the 1720s, and over 6,000 Africans by the 1760s. The West India Company took the largest number of captives from Keta, Klein Popo, Fida, Jaquin, Offra, Appa, and Patackerie on the Slave Coast, followed by the Gold Coast and the Dutch Loango-Angola Coast (modern Angola and the Republic of the Congo).

Leo Balai stared out over the moody waters beyond the walls of Fort Zeelandia. Somewhere out there to the east the *Leusden* got stuck. "It hit the sandbank," he told the dive team, "and that was the beginning of the end. Here, right here in front of us was where the *Leusden* was supposed to enter the Suriname River to sell the 'cargo'. Imagine, that two hundred to three hundred years ago, this place was all slave plantations. More than six hundred plantations with tens of thousands of slaves to make a profit for people who wanted to get rich. It was here where everything happened, where people were treated like cargo . . ."

From the urban comfort of Paramaribo, it was hard for Alannah, Kramer, and Kinga to imagine the picture Leo Balai was painting. Where he was about to take them would put the fear of God into the friends forever.

HENRY THE NAVIGATOR

It was in Portugal, not Holland, that the trickle of cash made by the slave trade turned into a 350-year torrent of riches. In the popular holiday destination of Lagos on the southwestern spear tip of Portugal, holidaymakers dream of cheap sun closer to home than the Mediterranean. The city has it all: romantic crumbling fortifications, dreamy rocky shores and sandy beaches near the Praia da Rocha, delicious seafood, luxury hotel resorts, and bottomless beer.

How many weekend stag and hen parties know, though, what lurks beneath the flagstones of party central? The Valle da Gafaria cuts through open land just outside Lagos's city walls. A few years ago, archaeologists were rushed in when developers building a new multistorey parking lot were stopped in their tracks. They had disturbed what no developer wants to hit, two ancient cemeteries. One was the city leper colony known from old maps. The other was undocumented, a grisly mass of urban waste thrown away centuries ago.

A stone's throw from the city's ancient harbor, into the six-meter-thick layer of trash sailors had slung the leftover garbage of long-distance sea voyages, from ships' smashed pots to the bones of fish, chicken, pigs, and goats. Littered among the maritime junk were 158 human skeletons, some violently thrown away, still shackled. A woman went to her grave hugging her baby. Rings, necklaces, and sharpened human teeth left no doubt where they once originated in far-off Africa.

At this very spot on August 8, 1444, Lançarote da Ilha, the royal tax collector for Lagos, returned home in six caravel ships crammed with 240 shackled captives taken from the Arguin Bank in Mauritania. Prince

Henry, the son of King John I, ordered the enslaved be paraded in a field near the port for all to cheer Portugal's preeminence. The waterfront was crowded with rubbernecking city folk taking in the exotic spectacle. Prince Henry on horseback pointed out which slaves he wanted as his royal one-fifth *quinto* (royal tax) entitlement for licensing the voyage. The Church was also there, raking in its own rightful one-twentieth of goods promised to the Order of Christ.

In his *Chronicle of the Discovery and Conquest of Guinea*, Gomes Eanes de Zurara described the astonishing birth of the Western slave trade that fateful day:

> Very early in the morning, by reason of the heat, the seamen began to make ready their boats, and to take out those captives, and carry them on shore . . . And these, placed all together in that field, were a marvelous sight; for amongst them were some white enough, fair to look upon, and well pro-portioned; others were less white like mulattoes; others again were as black as Ethiops, and so ugly, both in features and in body . . . some kept their heads low and their faces bathed in tears, looking one upon another; others stood groaning very dolorously, looking up to the height of heaven . . . others struck their faces with the palms of their hands, throwing themselves at full length upon the ground . . . to increase their sufferings still more, there now arrived those who had charge of the division of the captives, and who began to separate one from another, in order to make an equal partition of the fifths; and then was it needful to part fathers from sons, husbands from wives, brothers from brothers. No respect was shewn either to friends or relations, but each fell where his lot took him . . . the mothers clasped their other children in their arms, and threw themselves flat on the ground with them; receiving blows with little pity for their own flesh, if only they might not be torn from them.

African captives like this ended up dead in Lagos's Valle da Gafaria between 1420 and 1480. DNA analysis has shown how the Africans were

taken from the Bantu-speaking groups of West Africa. Born outside the
laws of Christendom, these men, women, and children were brutally
thrown into the city dump without a prayer, mortally weakened from
the horrors of the sea crossing or dying just after landing.

The exiled captives were never baptized, so their corpses were treated
no different than animals. Their souls could not be saved. Over the
desecrated site of their final resting places, Lagos's Pro Putting Garden
modern mini-golf course was built with joyful fountains, bridges, and
colorful sculptures of pink, green, and red dancing mother goddesses.

Father of the Slave Trade

The Africans found in the world's oldest slave cemetery were thrown
away because they were deemed to have no value. The transatlantic slave
trade was born in the shadow of the Valle da Gafaria. From here Portugal
seized the lion's share of slave riches for centuries. From Lagos, African
slavery and the globe's great sugar rush reached far out to Brazil, sucking
in the Dutch, Suriname, and the tragic sinking of the *Leusden*.

All in all, Portuguese slave traders shipped around 5.8 million Africans between the fifteenth and nineteenth centuries, roughly 50 percent
of the transatlantic traffic. And the full inhumanity of the machine all
began in the city square of Lagos, the lead port for importing Africans
between 1444 and 1473.

Dom Henrique, the Prince of Portugal from 1394 to 1460, and more
famously known as Henry the Navigator, is credited as the father of the
slave trade. For kickstarting Europe's overseas expansion, Henry is seen
as a heroic inventor, pioneering scientist, the ideal crusader and promoter
of the Catholic faith. Henry became the poster boy for Portugal's Golden
Age and the birth of the Age of Exploration. Public polls in Portugal and
North America included Henry the Navigator among the twenty-five
most important historical figures of the second millennium.

What Dom Henrique did and did not achieve is shrouded in mystery.
The truth may never be known after Portugal's archives in Lisbon were
destroyed in the great earthquake of 1755. History nevertheless honors
Henry as the founder, at windswept Sagres, just west of Lagos, of a

scientific citadel with a nautical school bustling with mathematicians, astronomers, cartographers, and instrument makers. The Englishman Samuel Purchas described in 1625 how Henry "caused one Master James, a man skillful in Navigation, and in Cards [charts] and Sea Instruments, to be brought into Portugal, there at his charge, as it were, to erect a school of Marineship, and to instruct his countrymen in that Mysterie."

Sweating over sea maps day and night, legend has it that at Sagres Prince Henry uncovered the hidden secret to long-distance seafaring. The Venetian explorer Cadamosto later wrote that the caravel ships of Portugal could travel anywhere. Africans were struck by eyes painted onto the bows of caravels. They were convinced these gave ships the vision to sail anywhere in the uncharted world.

Caravels with the unmissable square cross logo of the Order of Christ painted onto their sails were the ships of choice for crusading with West Africa. Large rectangular sails inclined at an angle on a mast allowed them to sail close to the wind, make headway under light winds and keep away from pirates. Crucially, because they were small ships of no more than forty to fifty tons, their shallow hulls made them perfect for maneuvering along and exploring the coast of Guinea's shallows and rivers.

In the words of Samuel Purchas, Prince Henry became "The true foundation of the Greatnesse, not of Portugall alone, but of the whole Christian World, in Marine Affairs . . ." The English poet and playwright Dr. Samuel Johnson later called him "the first encourager of remote navigation." Much of the Navigator's red-hot publicity is now thought to be overhyped. Triangular sails date back to the eighth century and the caravel existed in the thirteenth century. And there's no certainty Henry founded a nautical school at Cape Sagres at all. To many, Henry was little more than a pirate, slaver, and corrupt monarch. Whatever the truth, the Infanta Dom Henrique was the first major backer of a Western slave-trading expedition. With power, cash, and vision, he kicked off the deadly game for global colonial supremacy.

Fifty years after the first captives reached Lagos, Portugal was trafficking up to two thousand African captives a year through Oporto and Lisbon. Like in London, some were set to work in domestic service in the big cities. The Flemish traveler Nicolas Cleynaerts, tutor to Henry the Chaste and future king of Portugal, worried in the 1530s that

> Slaves swarm everywhere. All work is done by blacks and captive Moors. Portugal is crammed with such people. I should think that in Lisbon slaves, male and female, out-number freeborn Portuguese . . . Richer households have slaves of both sexes, and there are individuals who derive substantial profits from the sale of the offspring of their household slaves . . . they raise them much in the same way as one would raise pigeons for sale in the marketplace.

Lisbon boasted twelve slave markets by the mid–sixteenth century. Twenty years later, forty thousand people were enchained in Portugal.

Iberian Sugar

Most of the slaves seized in Portugal's crusading "just war" were set to work in sugar plantations on the island of Madeira. Sugar's stock was rising fast after being brought over from the Middle East with defeated Crusaders. Before becoming the greatest explorer of all time, Christopher Columbus had lived and married on Madeira, where he worked for an Italian firm in the sugar trade. When he sailed to the Caribbean in 1493, he took with him sugarcane cuttings as a symbol of Iberia's wealth.

Madeira became the largest producer of sugar in the Western world, by 1510 turning out 3,701 tons of white and brown granules. Sugar sold as far east as Constantinople and as north as England. Boom time had arrived. The Atlantic sugar rush brought vast bucks. But it was small fry compared to what was to come. When Portuguese hulls took sugarcane and technological expertise into its cash-cow colonies in Brazil, sugar turned into a monster. The world got addicted.

Turning up the heat on the global economy needed a level of man-power that had never been harnessed before. The clock ticked down on the ransacking of Africa.

Tracking down physical traces of Portugal's immense role in the slave trade is hard to do. So far only one Portuguese shipwreck tied to its transatlantic slaving has come to light. Which makes the world's earliest slave cemetery in Lagos all the more telling. But its story is hardly known. Thrill-seeking and playing golf have buried the city's inhumane past.

BOLTING THE HATCHES

Deep down the Maroni River it is difficult to see why Dutch merchants invested fortunes taking Suriname. The dense forest pushes all the way to the riverbanks. The foreboding interior feels full of demons.

In the wildest depths of the Wild Coast, Alannah, Kramer, and Kinga were heading to the town of Albina to meet Leo Balai, his Dutch marine archaeologist, Professor Jerzy Gawronski from the University of Amsterdam, and marine technology expert Steve Moore. From here they would time-travel in search of the *Leusden*, the Dutch trader that sunk with history's greatest loss of trafficked African life.

Palm trees bent above fine sandy beaches along the Maroni River, the border between Suriname and French Guiana. The water was already choppy and murky brown. There was no going back. Diving With A Purpose was all in. Dr. Gawronski is highly respected and experienced. He had worked on land and sea, recently excavating a treasure trove of trade goods under a new metro terminal construction site in Amsterdam. Underwater, Gawronski had been at the heart of projects from Spitsbergen in Norway to Nova Zembla in Russia, the Magalhães Straits in Chile, Sri Lanka, and Curaçao. But he had never found and saved a slave ship in a river.

Balai and Gawronski were in a rush. The *Leusden* had been lost to the world for too long. The ship—the wreck—should be a central pillar in new Dutch consciousness for a country where nobody wanted to confront the dark side of the human past.

DUTCH SHIPPING & WEST AFRICA

Between 1674 and 1740 the West India Company equipped 383 ships for the transport of slaves. Dutch slavers were adapted with a *diep verdeck*, a narrow tween deck between the lower and upper decks. This extra space held slaves and freed up the hold for cargo, food, supplies, and water.

The largest slave trade ships were flutes, pinnaces, and frigates thirty-three to thirty-six meters long, manned by forty-five to sixty sailors, armed with fifteen to twenty guns, and able to transport 600 slaves on average. The largest slave shipment trafficked by a West India Company trader was 952 Africans. Medium-sized frigates, yachts, and galiots, crewed by up to forty-five sailors and with ten cannons maximum, carried 400 slaves. Small barques and hookers had crews of up to thirty men and under ten guns that could carry 200 slaves per voyage. Average voyages sailing the triangular trade from Holland to West Africa, the New World, and home took 516 days.

Once in West Africa, trading voyages up and down the coast searching for trade goods and African human cargo varied from a few weeks to eight-month trips to the Bight of Benin and Biafra. The West India Company preferred fishing vessels like *buizen* (buses), *hoekers* (hookers), and *pinken* for coastal trading, manned by five to fifteen sailors and protected with one or two small cannons, a few muskets, machetes, and swords.

Dutch slave ships were obliged to sail in and out of Africa by way of the fort at Elmina. There captains made sure captives were healthy. Before leaving the Gold Coast a captain had to buy two "Negro Drums" and a wooden stick for the captives to drum as a distraction and entertainment during the crossing.

Abandon Ship

The *Leusden* was one of the last slave ships used by the Dutch West India Company. From the start, between its maiden voyage in 1719 until it sank, it was dedicated to the slave trade. In the fateful year of 1738, it was on its tenth slaving voyage. Through the years the *Leusden* trafficked 6,564 Africans, 1,639 of whom died at sea.

The final crossing was cursed. The captain died shortly after the trader docked at the Dutch fort of Elmina on the Gold Coast. A newly appointed commander, Joachim Outjes, was dispirited to find that stocks of captives were too low to fill the *Leusden* with "cargo" and make a quick turnaround. The eagerness of African kings and middlemen to deal with the Dutch had soured because of the low prices they offered. Whereas the West India Company bartered up to 200 guilders worth of goods for a captive, other Europeans went as high as 280 guilders. Plus, Dutch merchants had been found out for their underhand fobbing Africans off with "poor quality and broken goods."

Rather than wait, the *Leusden* headed 140 kilometers east to the Dutch trading post of Fort Crevecoeur near Accra in Ghana to search out a slave cargo where the Ashanti and Fante had been waging tribal wars. Still the *Leusden* only managed to find 200 Africans. Filling the hold turned out to be hard work. The slaver was forced to sail up and down the coast of Ghana for 192 days before closing the hatches on 700 Africans.

DUTCH TRADE WITH AFRICA

In the fort of Elmina in Ghana, the Dutch held 150–200 sorts of goods to barter with African peoples. Textiles manufactured in Europe, Asia, and Africa were most important at 50 percent of all stores. In the years 1727–1730, the West India Company sent 40,000 sheets of Dutch linen to the Gold Coast. Military stores, firearms, and gunpowder accounted for 12 percent of West India Company trade goods. In the first quarter of the 18th century the Company shipped 68,797 firearms and over 1.5 million pounds of gunpowder. Thirty-three percent was bad stock and dangerous. The Company made a 100 percent profit on firearms.

Around 900,000 pounds of cowrie shells were shipped to Europe from the Maldives Islands by the Dutch and English East India

Companies between 1700 and 1723 (11 percent of imported Dutch goods) to barter with West Africa. Dutch gin and French brandy were welcomed by Africans who also bought beer and wine (4 percent of Dutch imports). Large volumes of iron bars, metal pans, buckets, knives, and locks were imported, as well as luxury beads, trinkets, and mirrors.

As well as trafficking Africans, ivory accounted for 13 percent of West India Company exports to Holland. Between 1676 and 1731, three million pounds of ivory were shipped from Elmina to Europe to manufacture snuff boxes, fans, cutlery, medallions, and furniture inlays. The company exported 14,260 kilograms of gold from Ghana between 1676 and 1731. Out of Africa, Dutch ships also took home "Buenos Aires" hides, cayenne pepper, wax, gum, dyewood, lime juice, cardamom, ostrich feathers, copper, and live civet cats, the secretion from their anal glands used to make perfume.

The crew had every reason to hope their problems were now behind them. The voyage was blissfully smooth from Elmina outward to Suriname. The weather behaved and the captives' health held. Within forty-four days the *Leusden* was off Suriname—its quickest ever crossing.

The crew's luck ran out when, on December 29, 1737, the ship passed Devil's Island, off the coast of French Guiana. In the face of heavy winds, driving rain, and thick fog, the captain ran for the shore. When the weather cleared, the crew spotted a tip of land, which surely had to be Braamspunt at the head of the Suriname River.

A heavy rainstorm clouded over the sight of land once more, and the strong tide pushed the *Leusden* too close to the coast, where it bobbed uncomfortably offshore for hours, waiting for the outgoing tide to float out to the open sea. It never happened. At 4:00 P.M. on January 1, 1738, at a depth of just under six meters, the rudder hit a sandbank. Water flooded the cabin and gunpowder room. The pumps could not work fast enough to stop the *Leusden* from slowly sinking. The crew still had enough time to bolt down the hatches and sit out the night on top of the ship as it turned into a wreck. Seventy-three crew members then abandoned ship and sailed to Paramaribo in the *Leusden*'s launch and sloop. They never looked back.

Left behind in the hold were 664 African men, women, and children. When the slave quarters started flooding with water, the captives pushed higher up the ship to avoid drowning. With the sea at low tide, and the nearshore sandbanks dry and exposed, the Africans could easily have waded to shore and salvation. The Dutch crew had other plans. They made the astonishing decision to nail down the hatches, trapping hundreds of humans to die within sight of shore.

Nobody cared. The crew was more concerned about getting paid a 10 percent salvage award for saving a treasure chest with twenty-three kilograms of gold from the *Leusden*'s hold, recovered "with the greatest peril to their lives," so Captain Outjes reported. The officers and sailors found the time to salvage the ship's treasure chest but not their fellow man.

The tragic loss of the *Leusden* was forgotten. Captain and crew did not lose any sleep over the 664 souls they purposefully allowed to drown. For the Dutch West India Company, it was a minor irritation. In one act of bolting down the hatches, the *Leusden* committed the largest massacre at sea in the history of the transatlantic slave trade.

Mowing the Lawn

Up and down the mouth of the Maroni River, Jerzy Gawronski and Steve Moore have spent years searching for the wreck of the *Leusden* with Leo Balai. They knew it had to be close. This season Diving With A Purpose was adding more eyes and experience to pinpoint the wreck and expose the story to the world.

Gawronski helped the team carry their dive tanks into a small, narrow barge. The team was hunting the ancient Dutch ship not on a high-tech research boat boasting the latest gadgets, but from the same kind of vessel that had sailed these waters for ages. Only now a motor had been bolted onto its stern. Flat-bottomed hulls like these can ride high enough over the shifting sandbanks not to become another casualty.

"The *Leusden* is somewhere out there by the mouth of the Maroni River," Professor Gawronski was convinced. He pointed to where the river met the North Atlantic Ocean. "So, I invite you aboard and let's find it."

The boat chugged past a village of round, thatch-roofed huts lost to time. The branches of the forest trees waved, running all the way down the shore, inviting the divers to plunge in and resurrect the enslaved voices in the shallows.

At Galibi, the nearest village to the mouth of the Maroni River, the team set up camp. Over a worktable they started poring over historic maps that showed how the river's course and sandbanks had changed over time.

Gawronski reconstructed what he and Leo Balai thought was the final route of the confused ship.

"Okay guys," Jerzy began, getting serious. "With these historical maps, together with the crew's testimony, we were able to identify several target areas for the wreck of the *Leusden*. The ship arrived here around the 30th of December, 1737." The marine archaeologist tapped a map showing the coastline ninety-five kilometers east of the Maroni River, where the captain plotted a reading in the ship's log.

"They described that they followed the coast from the east and then early morning on the first of January they saw a river mouth," Jerzy continued. "There were very heavy rains, like a wall of water, very heavy winds. And then in the fog, they saw the corner of land. They hit a sandbank and got stuck, they lost the rudder and there was a massive hole."

In the confusing swirl of atrocious weather, the captain mistook the Maroni for the Suriname River. It was a catastrophic error. The hull opened up like a zipper and rapidly took on water.

"And at that point they knew there was no saving the ship?" Kinga asked.

"In the account," Gawronski clarified, "they called it a 'wreck.' Not a 'ship,' but a 'wreck.' In order to get an idea of what happened, we also have a map from that period. This is a map from 1777 indicating more or less the situation during the wreckage. And you see a number of sandbanks. And on one of these sandbanks, the ship must still be stuck."

The Dutch were excellent seafarers who pioneered early navigational equipment. Onto the 1777 map, their cartographers had inked precise details showing the contours of the sandbanks, their shape and location as they existed 244 years ago.

Kramer had been quiet all the way during the commute from Albina. He had watched the choppy waves and drain-water brown river. This was going to be like diving in pea soup, he realized.

"Jerzy, I'm wondering—with the silt and the currents going through—how that is going to affect the dive?" Kramer asked politely. Alannah screwed up her face and rubbed her chin.

"Well, in these circumstances, the visibility is reduced sometimes to zero because of the presence of all this silt floating in the water. But let's hope for the best," Gawronski replied unconvincingly, the wind already whipping his hair. Kramer was in for a tough shift.

"So, we won't know until we get out there, huh?" Kinga threw in, ever chipper.

"No . . . and it can change day by day," Jerzy added.

The team took once more to the water, this time in a slightly more stable boat.

Kinga summed up the plan to find the *Leusden*. "This river mouth is huge. Over three miles wide, so the first step in pinpointing the shipwreck is to scan the possible targets on the riverbed with a specialized metal detector. The mission now is to find a trail of metallic debris."

"Could be nails from the ship, ballast, guns, the anchors, of course. The captain used two or three anchors, and also a large amount of shackles to hold down the slaves," Jerzy explained.

Alannah helped deploy overboard into the murky soup a bright yellow Aquascan magnetometer. It looked more like a World War II artillery shell. The boat started towing the bright fish in its wake, meticulously and slowly "mowing the lawn." Hopefully its high sensitivity Fluxgate sensors would pick up the tiniest of metallic objects pinging off the seabed.

The team plowed back and forth over the square mile they had targeted as the last resting place of the *Leusden*. It was tedious but essential groundwork. The mission took days.

Unlike the Florida Keys and English Channel, both maritime highways for centuries, major sea trade off the Maroni River only started with the arrival of the Dutch in the early seventeenth century.

Kramer was optimistic despite the conditions. "There has never been much shipping activity in these waters," he pointed out. "So, if we find any sign of metal, that would strengthen our theory that this is the site of the underwater wreck."

Leo Balai watched the hunt unfold, resolute and strong. "The *Leusden* is so important for the history of the slave trade. We have to find it," he told the crew, keeping them motivated.

After five days surveying the waters, the team failed to pick up any signals on the Aquascan. It was a painful wake-up call for how hard it can be to track down wrecks that do not want to be found.

But then, as so often happens in archaeology, on the last day, everything changed in an instant.

From inside the boat's cabin, it was Steve Moore's job to guide the survey track lines and watch the profile of metallic bumps and lumps register on his laptop's software. As the boat reached the end of another grid line, he spotted something familiar.

"I think we got something . . ." Steve announced. "Yeah, yeah definitely. We are seeing some sort of target or something metallic down there. We need to pull it in and have a look." On the computer the graph showed a double low dip, registering a big metallic hit on the seabed.

The dive team was relieved. They finally had their purpose, their lead. The boat shut down its engines and swayed from side to side on the choppy water. It was time to get eyes on the prize and verify the target. It now looked like, almost three hundred years after the disastrous sinking of the *Leusden*, the crew could be floating right over the wreck.

TWISTED TONGUES

To make sense of what the Dutch were up to in Suriname means turning the spotlight on Brazil, the country where the slave trade began in earnest in 1440. Along the hilltops of Recife on the country's central east coast, the achingly beautiful scenery has not changed for five hundred years. Field after field of lush green sugarcane rolls as far as the eye can see. It was in this paradise that the torture of African slave labor first took hold in the New World. From these soils, enslavement encircled the Caribbean and on to Suriname.

Sugar factories have been part of Brazil's landscape since 1542. Today Black workmen, direct descendants of trafficked Africans, still cut the cane, now dressed in their favorite football team shirts. White supervisors on horseback keep a beady eye on their investment. Until now the best "machine" for cutting sugarcane is people. In Brazil sugar production reached new levels of efficiency and profit.

Just as Brazil is the biggest exporter of sugar in the world today, so it was ground zero for sugar destined for Europe's markets five centuries ago. For fifty years Holland and Portugal fought a relentless war to control global commerce. At stake, in what has been called the first true world war, was new overseas empires and earning the bragging rights to be the supreme superpower of the Western world.

Portugal sent the first sugar technician to Brazil in 1516 to oversee a sugar mill start-up. Within a decade you could buy Brazilian sugar in Lisbon and Antwerp. The experiment took root. More skilled experts were contracted from Portugal, Italy, Galicia in Spain, the Canary Islands, Belgium, and Madeira to turn Brazil into the West's newest cash cow. Plantings shipped from Madeira were grafted into the soil between São Vicente in the south and Pernambuco in the north, flat lands with fertile ground conveniently near the shore for export and covering four thousand square miles, three quarters the size of Connecticut. Production skyrocketed beyond the limits of the small island of Madeira, the former capital of sugar cultivation. From 1570 to 1585 the number of sugar factories in Brazil rose from 60 to 128 with Pernambuco and Bahia controlling three quarters of the country's output. Where a sugar mill on Madeira could turn out 15 metric tons of sugar a year, Brazilian mills bagged 130 tons.

At first, the Portuguese enslaved natives seized in what the Church called a "just war." The Indigenous people, though, were found to be poor workers, no doubt often deliberately. In any event, Indigenous people had no immunity to European diseases. Between 1492 and 1700, smallpox, chicken pox, and typhoid killed an estimated fifty-five million natives, or 90 percent of Indigenous people in the Americas. Some twenty-first-century climate scientists have suggested that the mass deaths and the resulting abandonment of agricultural land led to a "terrestrial carbon uptake," when the land was reclaimed by nature. Put simply, so many people died that this may have led to the Little Ice Age between the fourteenth and nineteenth centuries. The Europeans now had a problem. They needed cheap labor and they had to fill the hole left by the millions of dead. Enter the Africans.

Africans were the polar opposite of the Indigenous people of the Americas. They had been tried and tested in Portugal's sugar plantations on Madeira. Cane cutting took man and woman teamwork. The man cut and his companion bound the canes into faggots. Harsh quotas of around 4,200 canes had to be met every day or else. Conditions were ruthless. Failure to hit quotas was punished by slaves being scorched with hot wax, branded on the face or chest, or having their ears or noses chopped off. Sexual brutality was also common in Portuguese Brazil. The lucky ate food made from manioc flour, salt meat, fish, rice, and bananas, topped off with whale meat. The unfortunate swallowed whatever they could get their hands on. Even rats caught in sugarcane fields were boiled in cooking pots.

PLAGUE IN BRAZIL

Plague appeared on the Brazilian coast as a serious problem in 1559. Disease, probably smallpox, killed over six hundred enslaved Indigenous people in Espirito Santo the next year. Overall, an estimated thirty thousand perished. Father do Valle described children dying on their mothers' breasts for lack of milk, people so weak that they could not dig graves for the dead or collect water for the living. On some sugar plantations, ninety to one hundred slaves perished. In 1563, measles struck the weakened population. Another thirty thousand died. It was no accident that the importation of Africans began in the 1570s.

Many plantation masters cared little about their slaves' well-being, dismissing them as no better than "mute orangutans." But not everyone liked what they saw. Priests like the Italian Padre António Vieira detested the horrific conditions the Africans had to put up with, describing in 1633:

> And truly who sees in the blackness of night those tremendous furnaces perpetually burning; the flames leaping . . . the Ethiopians or cyclopses, bathed in sweat, as black as they are strong, feeding the hard and heavy fuel to the fire, and the tools they use to mix and stir them; the cauldrons, or boiling lakes, continually stirred and restirred, now vomiting froth, exhaling clouds of steam, more of heat than of smoke . . . the noise of the wheels and chains, the peoples the color of the very night working intensely and moaning together without a moment of peace or rest; who sees all the confused and tumultuous machinery and apparatus of that Babylon can not doubt though they may have seen Vesuvius or Mount Etna that this is the same as Hell.

By the time Brazil's pure-as-snow end product was packed, it was welcomed in Europe as the most prized commodity on earth. Already by 1625 almost fourteen thousand tons of sugar headed to the West a year, its prices marked up 60 percent higher than in Brazil. Even during the country's eighteenth-century gold rush, the value of Brazilian sugar exports exceeded all other commodities. From Brazil the sugar industry was copied across Barbados and the Caribbean. Sweetening coffee and tea became an inescapable craze of daily Western life. African slaves continued to be shackled and shipped to Brazil until 1855.

New Holland

For all the profit that the slave trade generated, there was an unimaginable loss. A loss counted in murdered Africans and wrecked ships. After jealously watching Portugal rake in colossal profits in Europe's great cities, Amsterdam decided to get in on the act. In 1623, the Dutch sent out war fleets to Brazil. All were repelled until, seven years later, sixty-seven ships and seven thousand soldiers took Olinda and Recife. Amsterdam now planted a flag in the sweet soils of New Holland.

Portugal had trafficked one hundred thousand Africans to its Brazil plantations in the first quarter of the seventeenth century. Now the Dutch duplicated its success. One hundred and sixty-six sugar mills were turning in Dutch Brazil by 1639. All Holland needed to power up its foothold in the Americas was an enchained army. The answer to Johan Maurits, the prince of Nassau-Siegen and governor of Dutch Brazil, was to try and capture Luanda, Portugal's slave market in Angola. A fleet of twenty-one ships set out. Without African slaves, Brazil's economy would be doomed.

In May 1641, Luanda and the great Portuguese slave port on the island of São Tomé were in Dutch hands. The Dutch West India Company was at the peak of its powers. It planned to ship to Brazil fifteen thousand slaves a year, aged fifteen to thirty-six. The Dutch West India Company reckoned the slave trade to Brazil should rake in six million guilders a year. Sugar and slaves were the richest prize on earth.

Even though the lowlanders were all too swiftly thrown out of Brazil in 1654, they kept a chokehold over slave trafficking by dominating former Portuguese lands in West Africa, including the jewel in Lisbon's crown, the mighty fort of Elmina in modern Ghana. Portuguese Brazilian slavers planning to trade on the Guinea Coast were forced to pay a 10 percent toll on the value of their cargo to Dutch authorities.

Down the decades, the Dutch would traffic around five hundred thousand slaves to the Americas, making it the fifth largest trader in slaves after Portugal, Britain, France, and Spain. It was after the loss of Brazil that Dutch merchants turned to nearby Suriname to grow their sugar and coffee ambitions.

New Blacks City

From a small business in the town of Lagos in Portugal, the slave trade became a worldwide moneyspinner, creating cities like Rio de Janeiro. It may surprise people, but only 4 percent of all enslaved Africans were sent to North America. The Caribbean received 36 percent. Fourteen percent went to Spanish America. But, between 1560 and 1852, 46 percent of the total—4.8 million Africans—arrived in Brazil.

In these years Rio de Janeiro was distastefully known as the "Black City." A graphic memory of the capital's shamed past came to light when Rio was being developed for the 2016 Olympics. Fast and furious construction work in the port area of Valongo, the Long Valley, uncovered the old city wharf where captive Africans first landed in the Americas. Archaeologists discovered a historic site covered with the memories Africans brought with them: tobacco pipes, beads, rings, magical cowrie shells from the Gulf of Guinea, good luck charms, anthropomorphic stones, and crystals. The dock formed part of a large slave quarters, including the quarantine station where captives infected with contagious diseases were locked up, and the Cemetery of Pretos Novos ("New Blacks"), where the victims of abusive sea voyages and the diseases they caught during crossings were discarded as worthless.

The cemetery itself came to light by chance when a young couple bought a new house and began home improvements. Digging in the foundations turned up human bones. And then more and more bones. Their home had been built on the cemetery of the New Blacks where Africans fresh off the boat were buried. Most had died on landing after forty-five to sixty days crossing the Middle Passage. To begin with, the bodies were laid to rest in orderly graves. Space quickly ran out as the dead reached unmanageable numbers. The cemetery deteriorated into an unmarked mass grave. Then, Rio's residents started using it as a general garbage dump.

When the smell got too bad, the locals burned down the garbage heap, and then the process started all over again, filling it up with discarded Africans and trash. Over thirty thousand Africans ended their lives in a random hellhole in the ground. Just like in Lagos, the enslaved of no economic value were cast off in the easiest and cheapest way possible.

Valongo's history fascinated the archaeologists. They immediately knew that the wharf was the setting for one of the greatest crimes in humanity. In the shadow of this place of unspeakable suffering, the dig's lead archaeologist, Tania Andrade Lima, wrote how

> We took Valongo out of the ground with our heart in our hands, with great respect and deep emotion. Considered one of the most notable places of memory of the African dias-pora outside of Africa itself . . . Valongo was understood as a location that encapsulates memories of pain and struggle for survival in the history of the ancestors of Afro-descendants.

The death and discarding on land and sea of millions of Africans was for most Europeans an acceptable by-product of profiting in billions of pieces of gold.

BONE CRUSHERS

Dawn broke over the Suriname River. The water ran slack and flat. The midmorning wind was yet to stir. At first light the locals were heading to work, crossing the broad river by ferry, carrying shopping baskets and pushing mopeds to scoot off to the office back on the other bank. Alannah, Kramer, and Kinga were commuting in the opposite direction, scouring the seabed off Suriname's fertile forests. Somewhere out there Leo Balai was certain lay the resting place of the long-lost *Leusden*, a Dutch trader sunk with the greatest loss of enslaved life in the history of the Netherlands. Blinding silver rays of sun lit up the water. Maybe it was a good omen from the spirits of the past.

In a narrow, motorized barge, the dive team slowly traveled upriver, away from the Atlantic Ocean. The Suriname River is vast. The explorers felt like insignificant specks caught between forest and water.

Leo Balai took the opportunity to remind the team about the *Leusden*'s final hours. "The ship was stuck on the sandbank and water came in. They tried to mend it, to prevent the water from coming in, but it didn't stop. The captain decided the ship was lost. He also decided that the 'cargo' was lost. The captives were of no value anymore. The 664 Africans who perished could have survived, but the captain had a different idea."

Diving With A Purpose was heading away from the sea inland to try and make sense of the best-case fate of the *Leusden*'s African captives if they had made it to Suriname alive. They would see where and how the Dutch manufactured huge profits.

"I want to show you what was supposed to be the final destination of the enslaved Africans on board the *Leusden*," Balai explained. "Around this whole territory there were slave plantations. And such a creek was essential to take the sugar and the coffee to the river and then to Paramaribo and transport it to the Netherlands and Amsterdam to sell."

Looking at the waterway running over the horizon, Kinga started to visualize how these shores once bustled with plantations. "So, these were the highways basically?" she asked.

Not only were these waters highways, Leo Balai confirmed, but what looked like a river was actually a canal hand dug by thousands of slaves over a hundred miles all the way to the Atlantic Ocean.

"If you look around you can't imagine that there were thousands of Black people living over here, died over here, were massacred sometimes over here because they had to make sugar and coffee," Leo observed. "Sugar was the curse of Black people, because Europeans wanted sugar."

The creek started to narrow. Branches hung over the water, keeping outside eyes away from the secrets abandoned in the interior. The riverbank was densely overgrown. Nature had reclaimed the past. A boa constrictor watched the divers sweep by, uncurled its body, and licked its lips but could not be bothered to move out of the sun and grab a juicy meal.

"So, nature is covering up the crime," Kramer whispered.

The team pushed deeper into the outback, bent over to stop being hit by trees overgrowing the creek.

Leo pointed out that once "This place was flatland, with sugar canes. Thousands of slaves working day and night."

"This was all flat, clear, no jungle?" a shocked Kinga exclaimed.

"No jungle," the Dutch scholar confirmed. "The slave owners were so inventive to stop the slaves from running away that they planted cactuses around the plantation so you couldn't get in or out."

The Suriname Trade

By the time the *Leusden*'s captain bolted down its hatches to deny the African captives any chance of escape, the once mighty Dutch West India Company was a shadow of its former glory. Its powerful grip over the Africa trade had crumbled. The battle for colonies and endless wars against Spain and Portugal in the Atlantic had exhausted the company's capital and took it near to bankruptcy. All Dutch commerce with Africa was opened to free traders from October 1734.

With the loss of New Brazil, Suriname was key to a range of agricultural wealth. Only in Suriname, Berbice, and Essequibo in Guiana did the West India Company hang onto its monopoly. In particular, it was contracted to deliver at least 2,500 slaves a year to the plantations owned by the Sociëteit van Suriname, a corporation run by the city of Amsterdam, the Amsterdam Chamber of the West India Company, and the aristocratic Van Aerssen van Sommelsdijck family. The company managed to ship 60,800 Africans to Suriname between 1674 and 1740.

By 1713, in its 171 factories, Suriname grew a wealth of tropical goods, not just sugar, but coffee, cacao, and cotton. By the late eighteenth century, the colony was one giant factory inhabited by five thousand European masters and seventy-five thousand slaves.

To feed the isolated colony, North America was a vital lifeline, sending four thousand ships to Paramaribo over 112 years. US traders sold building materials, household supplies, sheep, pigs, and geese to Suriname. Horses, needed to turn the heavy stones that crushed the sugarcane, were a vital overseas commodity. Six hundred horses were shipped to Suriname every year from New York, Connecticut, Massachusetts, and Rhode Island at the time when the *Leusden* sank. The American supply ships were known as "horse jockeys." Sadly, 36 percent of the horses died during the crossings, washed overboard from upper decks.

Sugar remained the king of Suriname's exports for two centuries, reaching twenty million pounds a year in the 1720s. By the time the *Leusden* set sail on its final voyage, the coffee beans first cultivated in Suriname rivaled sugar. Exports averaged more than 1.5 million pounds in the 1730s.

Silent Witness

The narrow barge veered down a tight creek off the Suriname River, just a few meters wide. The water was completely flat, the trees and bushes untamed. It felt as if no one had traveled these waterways for decades. All Alannah could make out were capuchin and red howler monkeys hooting, grunting, and jumping between trees. The wild jungle felt menacing. Humans had no right to be here. Kramer peered into the thick green wilderness and wondered what he was doing miles away from the sea where he should be searching for the *Leusden*.

The divers made landfall in the middle of nowhere. A pale green katydid sat patiently awaiting its next dinner of flies. The friends strolled uncertainly down an earthen snake track, nervously keeping their ears peeled for the forest's crocodiles, lancehead snakes, panthers, and jaguars. A mysterious wind blew through the leaves, sending shivers down the travelers' spines. Leo Balai sliced away foreboding undergrowth with his machete.

The cactus fence that Dr. Balai had mentioned, guarding the rainforest's interior, started to thin out. In the middle of the jungle, Diving With A Purpose stumbled onto what Leo brought them away from their ocean prize to see. The intended final destination of the *Leusden*'s 664 drowned captives.

Two ruined brick columns veered out of the wild forest undergrowth. Emerging out of the jungle, the team were suddenly confronted by giant, rusting monuments to a now dead age. Nearby, iron wheels that once turned a sugar mill stood rusting in the open air. Collapsed roofs and walls littered the ground next to an overturned oven.

"This is huge! What is it?" Alannah asked.

Leo Balai rested a soft hand on the mill teeth and explained that it was part of an abandoned sugar factory. "These are silent witnesses of an enormous crime," he continued. "You had hundreds of people working over you; some of them at the plantation to cut the cane. And then you have the people who work in the factory to process the cane. Imagine yourself being a slave over here, then you can see how horrible it was. Get up in the morning, work eighteen hours a day, seven days a week. Every mistake you make, the whip comes out."

The team could almost hear the cries of the enslaved Africans. Somebody had spent a small fortune investing in this factory of death and profit. Suriname's sugar estates, divided into squares, covered five hundred to six hundred acres. Some were staffed with up to four hundred slaves.

Kramer stared in disgust at the atrocity, failing to process the sense behind such brutal architecture. Anger and sadness coursed through his veins. A grim look crossed his face. What was worse, drowning on the *Leusden* or being led to a harrowing life making sugar?

Kramer knew all too well the fate the exiled could expect. Just to make sure, he asked, "So the life expectancy of an African here was about eight years?"

Leo confirmed that slaves forced to work on Suriname's sugar plantations lived an average of eight to ten years. And then it was over. Another 14 percent did not even make it, dying at sea in the hands of Dutch slavers.

Kramer, sensing the horrific living conditions of the ancestors, tried to control his emotions bubbling to the surface. "Alright, I am trying to imagine this, right?" he thought out loud. "You get captured in Africa and then once you are here . . ."

"You get branded," Leo added, tight-lipped but wanting to paint the full picture.

Kramer closed his eyes and took slow breaths before continuing in a soft whisper. "You get branded, right, bought and then tortured for eight years in a sugar plantation, and then you die."

All around the divers' feet lay scattered the debris of despair and destruction, the loose change left over from the eighteenth century's biggest moneymaker. Iron wheel cogs no longer turned, the oven was cold, and the pistons pumped no more. But the bitter taste of the sugared savagery still felt raw.

Kinga pulled the discussion back to the here and now. She needed help understanding the physical ruins at her feet. "What did all of this look like?" she asked. "What are all these pieces? We are looking at skeletons."

By the 1730s two great arm-shaped regions greedily enveloped the northern and western reaches of the Suriname River. A map drawn in 1734 shows an astonishing spiderweb of five hundred Dutch plantations clustered between the town of Paramaribo and along the Suriname and Commewijne Rivers. The estates bore Dutch, German, and French names, many perverse in hindsight. The slaves who broke their backs in the plantations of La Paix, La Liberté, and Nieuwe Hoop enjoyed no "peace," nor "freedom," nor chances of "new hope."

Alannah, Kramer, and Kinga walked past the engine, which lay shattered on the ground. Nearby was the oven that once melted cane juice. The most important part of the factory was the press. It was into this crusher that raw sugarcane was fed by armies of enslaved Africans until its juices ran free. This was a dangerous piece of equipment, especially if your hand got trapped inside.

DANGERS OF SUGAR MILLS

From Captain J. G. Stedman, *Narrative, of a Five Years' Expedition, Against the Revolted Negroes of Surinam, in Guiana . . . from the Year 1772 to 1777 . . . Volume I* (London, 1796). "So very dangerous is the work of those negroes who attend the rollers, that should one of their fingers be caught between them, which frequently happens through inadvertency, the whole arm is instantly shattered to pieces, if not part of the body. A hatchet is generally kept ready to chop off the limb, before the working of the mill can be stopped. Another danger is, that should a poor slave dare to taste that sugar which he produces by the sweat of his brow, he runs the risk of receiving some hundred lashes, or having all his teeth knocked out by the overseer. Such are the hardships and dangers to which the sugar-making negroes are exposed."

"When your hand gets stuck in the machine," Leo Balai was forced to spell out, "the only thing they did was to chop it off. Because they couldn't, wouldn't, stop the machine . . ."

Far away from London, Amsterdam, Lisbon, Paris, and Madrid a 24/7 world had developed to feed Europe's great capitals with coffee sweetened with must-have sugar. Nothing was allowed to get in the way of profit. Lost limbs were all in a day's work. The next victim in line simply walked forward, risking life and limb.

"There was always someone around here with a machete," Leo told the team.

"Someone stood here with a machete, just in case that happened," Kinga understood.

"Just in case, and it happened often because the people worked sixteen to eighteen hours a day and you get tired. And a mistake with such a machine often happens. That is the price of sugar, of course," Dr. Balai concluded.

Alannah saw the big picture. The Africans enslaved on the *Leusden* were in a lose-lose position. Death at sea or die worked to the bone? "And the Africans on the *Leusden*, they didn't even give them this chance to come here or try and live their eight years of life expectancy or to get away. They were murdered because the captain took a wrong turn. They weren't even worth the chance."

Alannah's voice trailed off. After seeing the workplace expected of African slaves in Suriname and hearing about their living conditions, the divers were even more desperate to track down the lost Dutch slaver and expose its horror story.

SWEET TOOTH

Transporting millions of slaves across the Atlantic took a tremendous amount of resources and money. How did these gigantic logistics make financial sense to Europeans and how did they balance the books? The answer lies in the bottom of a coffee cup.

In the first half of the seventeenth century, a commercial craze shook the civilized world. The humble berry discovered by an Ethiopian goatherder after his flock turned frisky chewing the bean in the wild became a $100 billion annual industry. After coffee at first stopped worshippers from falling asleep in mosques, coffeehouses opened across the Near East from Cairo to Constantinople. Sipping bitter black water was an expected sign of Turkish hospitality. By 1630 coffeehouses were go-to places for people from all walks of life to gossip, talk news, and make business deals across the Ottoman Empire.

The exotica of the "Orient" caught on fast in Britain after Parliament allowed Turks and Jews to trade in the kingdom. London's first coffeehouse, its doors opened in 1652, was the brainchild of a Christian Turk called Pasqua Rose who immigrated to London with an English merchant. Everyone loved Pasqua's coffee. So he set up a stall in a shed in the churchyard in St. Michael, Cornhill. Business boomed, and the shed was replaced by the capital's first coffeehouse just around the corner from the Royal Exchange in Saint Michael's Alley, the heart of commerce in the City of London. Overnight, copycat shops appeared. By 1663 London's punters could choose from eighty-three coffeehouses, and 550 by 1740. The forest-fire spread of coffee drinking was helped by Oliver Cromwell, the Lord Protector of Britain's war on fun. His Puritan party frowned on the theater, beer, and wine, and stooped as low as to ban Christmas. But Cromwell allowed coffee drinking as a diversion from all the other losses.

Coffee may have been prohibited in the Ottoman East for its drug-like intoxication, and King Charles II of England unsuccessfully tried to ban the drink in 1785 too, but Pope Clement VIII gave it a divine blessing. When Italian merchants presented him with a cup in 1581, he was hooked. As much as his priests pointed out that it was invented by infidel Muslims, the leader of the Catholic Church conveniently replied that "This Satan's drink is so delicious that it would be a pity to let the infidels have exclusive use of it. We shall cheat Satan by baptizing it."

Instead of profits flooding into Saracen pockets, England's East India Company started promoting tea over coffee, which it could better control. Tea was already being sipped in London by the 1650s, but mainly as medicine for the elite pockets of the famous, like the diarist Samuel Pepys. British tea drinking exploded after 1704 as scientists, medical experts, and fashionistas heralded the genius of taking a tea break. By 1767 Britain had seven million pounds of tea in its warehouses.

The obsession with tea created one of the most extraordinary social and cultural revolutions imaginable. Leaves shipped 10,000 miles were blended with sugar exported 5,000 miles. The sweet white crystals had been processed by Africans trafficked against their will 3,790 miles across the Atlantic.

Into bottomless cups serving coffee, tea, and cocoa, mountains of sugar was poured. All four addictive must-have products were shipped west through the hands of African slaves sweating in Brazil and Suriname. Sugar's volume and profit are hard to visualize. Addiction to the sweet tooth began on the side tables of the high and mighty. A French ambassador described the teeth of sugar lover Queen Elizabeth I as "very yellow and unequal . . . Many of them are missing so that one cannot understand her easily when she speaks quickly."

Bad teeth and sugar were not just a British complaint. Louis XIV of France, the Sun King, ruled without a tooth in his head. All of them had fallen out by the age of forty. The French were said to heap so much sugar into their coffee cups that spoons could stand up on their own. By 1800 sugar was one of life's pleasurable essentials.

The chain of manufacture that started with seizing and trafficking humans in West Africa was a vital cog in the making of the modern world, and the coffee shop was at its center. The insurance industry was born on the banks of the River Thames in Lloyd's Coffee House. Coffee shops doubled up as libraries and became places to read newly invented newspapers and discuss the politics of the day at a time when the Puritains' thought police were everywhere.

Coffeehouses were much more than places to drink: they were places to socialize, share information, read, and make deals. Sugar and coffee spawned modern polite society in spaces that broke down social barriers. Rich and poor rubbed shoulders. For the price of one penny, any man could enter and enjoy. And so coffeehouses became known as "penny universities." Playwrights and writers like Jonathan Swift and Samuel Pepys favored certain establishments. Men of fashion and young adventurers had their favorites. Families had their own local coffee shops.

Coffee was not to everyone's taste. Some women hated what the bean did to their men, complaining that "we poor Souls sit mopeing all alone till Twelve at night, and when at last they come to bed smoakt like Westphalia Hogs-head we have no more comfort of them, than from a Shotten Herring or dryed Bulgrush; which forces us to take up this Lamentation." The lobbyists demanded coffee be banned to make sure of a "return of old strengthening Liquors of forefathers and Lusty Heroes to improve women's interest and replenish the race." Men seemed to prefer coffee and manly fellowship to making babies. Other women made hay on the back of coffee and sugar, running and working in shops. Moll King's café became an infamous den of prostitution.

Ironically, it was on the tea tables of elegant ladies, a centerpiece for intimate meetings and polite discussion, that the tide against sugar and the slave trade turned. *An Address to the People of Great Britain on the Utility of Refraining from the Use of West India Sugar and Rum*, written by William Fox in 1791, stirred the waters by claiming that ladies' sugar-sweetened tea was tainted by the blood of African slaves. The accusation hit a raw nerve.

Fox, a publicity genius, warned his genteel audience that each pound of West Indian sugar contained two ounces of African flesh. His pamphlet sold over 250,000 copies in more than twenty editions. The poet and opium addict Samuel Taylor Coleridge angrily denounced the murder of colonial slaves so that "fine Ladies and Prostitutes' might be fashionably out-fitted as they gathered around the British tea table."

After reading Fox's broadside, around half a million British abstained from sugar taken in coffee and tea and eaten in desserts, bread, porridge, and puddings. Sugar and the slave trade had turned sour.

DEAD SILENCE

On the Tiger Bank at the entrance to the Suriname River, Jerzy Gawronski and Steve Moore had managed to nail down a set of coordinates as the potential location where the *Leusden* was wrecked and its human cargo of Africans drowned. Suriname may be blessed with no winter, a strong attraction for its pale Dutch overlords, but that did not make these waters any more alluring. The swirling ocean still looked pea soup green rather than tropical blue.

On a digital map, Jerzy and Steve had plotted a red grid around part of the Tiger Bank where the Aquascan magnetometer registered a big spike above something unnatural, something metallic on or under the seabed.

"We can see here the target we just got," Steve pointed out on a graph, taking off his glasses to peer at his laptop screen. "There's two passes here, identical! So that is a definite hit." The team surveyed the area repeatedly to make sure their eyes did not deceive them.

Jerzy looked on, hand on chin, wondering whether he could dare to dream. Leo Balai was tight-lipped. Nobody on earth had researched the *Leusden* as deeply. In his mind's eye he could imagine the ship's last hours and the panic onboard as the African captives realized they were being abandoned. Finding the *Leusden* would be epic, the crowning achievement of his life's work. For the first time in days, the mood lifted over the heavy weight pressing down on the divers' shoulders. Was the *Leusden* finally ready to give up its ghosts?

As ever, Kramer was figuring the angles, wondering what could positively identify the wreck. "I don't want to get ahead of myself," he cautioned, "but we do know that the *Leusden* dropped more than one anchor, and it was carrying a number of cannons." These kinds of sunken artifacts were exactly what could register metallic hits like Steve and Jerzy had found.

Steve's experience matching magnetic targets to wrecked finds told him the team was on the right track. "That's definitely something iron, an anchor, a few cannons, a cluster of shackles," he tried to convince the crew. "It could be something really big and really deep or it could be something not so big just under the surface."

Kinga was sold. "Okay got it. So, we're in the right place," she hoped. "Finally, we have a definite target."

Steve's energy was sky-high. "Yes, the right target, the right signal, the right everything."

Diving With A Purpose started preparing their gear. Their date with destiny had arrived. This was why they crossed the Atlantic and spent days surveying miles of ocean in search of a small patch of wreckage of immense historical importance. Kramer strapped his buoyancy vest to a white dive tank: even if the water was murky, his friends surely would be able to spot him.

Kinga checked her dive computer. If the visibility was poor, she would need to rely on it to make out north from south.

As the senior diver on the expedition, the plan was for Kramer to head down first. You did not need to be a master dive instructor to appreciate that these waters were incredibly dangerous. Kramer would need to overcome strong currents, low visibility, and then hope not to come face to face with venomous stingrays feeding on the riverbed. He had drawn the short straw. Still, scouring the seabed was a duty, he felt. He owed it to the *Leusden*'s drowned voices.

Kramer pulled on his signature gray-and-black-hooped wetsuit. Somewhere down there, Captain Joachim Outjes and his crew locked up 664 Africans and threw away the key. Now the divers were back to pick the lock.

Alannah spelled out what Kramer had signed up to. "During the dive, there will be no direct communication between Kramer and us," she explained. "So, a rope is attached to him and, in case of an emergency, we can pull him up."

Diving With A Purpose was going old school. The conditions were too hazardous for everyone to dive. They could all get lost in the soup or swept away by the fast-running currents. Everyone knew what the security alarm of a rope meant. The topside team would need to pull Kramer out of the Maroni River fast if he ran into trouble like being menaced by those stingrays or getting tangled in fishermen's nets.

Kramer was focused on the task at hand. "It's just me, but it's not. I am sensing the souls of six hundred-plus and I want to find them," he said out loud. There was no way he was going to back out, come hell or high water.

Steve Moore had devised an old-school communications system using the rope line. "Kramer, let's just go over the signals," he said. "One long pull: return the signal, 'I'm okay, are you okay?' Two pulls: 'I am coming up.' Or four pulls: 'There's a problem, coming up,' or 'We have a problem, get me up.'"

Kramer was only half listening. He was desperate to come up with good news, to tell the team, "They're here. We've found them; we've done what Dr. Balai called us for." Then Diving With A Purpose, Leo Balai, Jerzy Gawronski, and Steve Moore could try and give the lost Africans peace and hopefully, on some level, a proper burial.

The shallow-bottomed barge bobbed precariously from side to side like a drunken sailor as Kramer gingerly clambered over a blue steel ladder in the stern. Along the side, the boat's name was written in black paint, *Maranatha*, a biblical reference to 1 Corinthians: "Our Lord has come." Would the *Leusden*'s 664 enslaved get divine justice today?

Just as Kramer was about to drop into inner space, Steve added more insult to the danger of the dive. "Kramer, this is for sweeping on the bottom for any stingrays," he said, dropping a wooden pole down to him. The lead instructor for Diving With A Purpose had the lowest form of tech to protect him. Kramer followed the line of the *Maranatha*'s hull to the bow and then dropped down.

Time stood still. Kramer's air bubbles vanished. Everyone held their breath.

In his mind, Leo Balai played out the West India Company ship's final minutes. The *Leusden* had hit a sandbank and was sinking in the river mouth. At that moment the captain made a fateful decision. He ordered the sailors to nail down the hatches, in an instant signing the death warrant for 664 humans. To make sure, the sailors sat on the hatches all night.

By morning, all the Africans below deck were dead. They could easily have been saved. Instead, they drowned in shallow waters in sight of land. The captain and crew took to the lifeboats and made it safely to shore. Leo Balai shuddered. The screams of the forgotten souls haunted his dreams.

Why did the *Leusden*'s crew choose death over life? Why not simply unlock the hatches and let the enslaved make a run from the sinking ship? What did the captain have to lose?

The fateful decision of 1738 made little financial or humanitarian sense. If the West India Company planned to cash in an insurance policy on the ship's "cargo," letting the Africans sink may have had a despicable logic. It would have meant less paperwork and no need to organize a costly and dangerous posse to hunt them down in Suriname's rainforest.

Because they were classed as "valuable and perishable" cargo, slaves were insured in Genoa, Rome, and Barcelona from the fifteenth century and Antwerp and Holland by 1592. Private Dutch companies like the Middelburgse Commercie Compagnie insured hulls and cargo separately. General maritime insurance policies signed in Amsterdam covered losses caused by unexpected events at sea, such as storms, fire, and piracy. But when slaves escaped or revolted, marine insurers often refused to pay out claims. Just uncontrollable perils were covered. Slave insurrections were thought to be preventable.

In any case, the West India Company did not insure its captive human cargos. The *Leusden*'s hull was insured for ten thousand Dutch guilders and its goods for forty thousand guilders. The captain knew that the ship was old and that he could recoup most of its losses anyway. More to the point, his aim may have been to save his own hide. If he let the enslaved swim for it, they might have overpowered the crew, or worse. But he wasn't looking for a solution, not even for the children.

INSURING THE SLAVE TRADE

The question of "damage" caused by slave uprisings was heavily debated in Amsterdam. On December 17, 1750, the enslaved Africans on board the *Middelburgs Welvaren* revolted after the African coast was no longer in sight. To put down the revolt, the crew locked down the captives in the ship's hold and closed all openings to limit their view. As a result, 231 Africans suffocated.

When the ship returned home to Middelburg in 1751, an insurance claim was issued. The failed revolt led to an angry debate between the insurer, Servaas Bomme, and shipowner Jan De Munck. Rather than question the morality of the mass murder, Bomme and De Munck argued about "the damage," the reimbursement per murdered African, and who was responsible. In the end it is believed the insurer paid out.

After half an hour, Kramer slowly surfaced. Relief flooded the *Maranatha*.

Steve could not contain his hope. "How was it?" he asked.

"All blacked out . . ." Kramer said, his mouthpiece hardly spat out. As he slowly climbed up the boat's ladder, he shared his experience. The team pressed close to catch his breathless words. "Can't see a thing down there. I was feeling around, to see if I could feel something down there. Really didn't feel anything, right . . . just sandy and black."

Back onboard, Kramer started his return from the past to the present. He popped off his face mask and turned it backward. Even with eyes in the back of his head there was no seeing anything in the Maroni River's zero visibility. Sand from the Atlantic Ocean and the same soils where sugar and coffee once grew washed down from the rainforest, mixed together into an impenetrable gloom.

Thinking back to the sea bottom, Kramer told the team, "This is a murder scene and the souls of over six hundred Africans are down there. So, on some level, you want to feel like you can hear them calling to you, right? But it was just silence. Dead silence."

Skies and seas were overcast and not going to improve any time soon. The only way to ground-truth if the magnetometer had truly found the *Leusden* would be to dredge the seabed and uncover what lay below. If Diving With A Purpose was at the right spot, they might end up disturbing and bringing up the bones of the dead from the river bottom.

Directly below them they felt in their own bones the final resting place of the murdered and unnamed 664 Africans. Collectively, the team decided against dredging. The best decision was to let the dead rest. The divers and archaeologists would come again. Hope for better conditions.

As the *Maranatha* returned back to shore, Alannah found one image spinning around and around in her mind. Had the Africans been set free to flee into the surrounding jungle, could they have survived?

Before moving onto the next slave wreck, Leo Balai had one more secret to share with the team.

FREEDOM FIGHTERS

Leo Balai did not want the hunt for the *Leusden* to end on a low. The story of all Africans trafficked between West Africa and Suriname did not end badly. Thousands took their fate in their own hands. Leo also wanted to show the divers, show the world, that if the captain of the *Leusden* had shown enough compassion to unlock the hatches and let the captives swim for it, they could have sought asylum deep in Suriname's forest.

A red dawn shone down on the bones of the *Leusden*. The rising sun shimmered off the flat water. Palm trees stood motionless and trusting. The dive team's mood was subdued but they had high hopes for the future. The atrocious tale of the *Leusden* was out in the open, remembered.

Leo Balai was taking the team to one final place, called Akalikondre in the region of Marowijne, a Maroon village, fifty-four miles east of Paramaribo. "There is something more I want to show you," he winked.

"And the Maroons are escaped slaves?" Kinga asked.

"I call them 'freedom fighters,'" Leo corrected, "because they fought the plantation owners, killed them, went away, took people with them. Went into the woods and started new communities."

The deeper the river barge chugged down the creeks, the more canoes and people the team spotted along the banks. Behind a picture-perfect tropical sandy beach, hidden behind the trees, wooden shacks appeared, home to descendants of slaves who escaped Suriname's plantations. Long after the Dutch went home, the Maroons stayed on, carving out an existence in one of the transatlantic slave trade's great survival stories.

The Maroons got their name from the Spanish word *cimarron*, meaning "cattle gone wild in the bush." Fed up with miserable living conditions and sexual exploitation, Suriname's enslaved Africans often rose up in rebellions, strikes, suicides, and sabotage. The freedom fighters who escaped built remote villages above waterfalls in terrain that Europeans could not reach, but reminded the captives of their tribal homelands. Every year the Maroons cut down and burned part of the forest, then replanted the charcoal-fertilized soils with rice, corn, yams, plantains, beans, peas, sweet potatoes, okra, peppers, and sugarcane. There the six tribes of Saramaka, Ndyuka, Matawai, Paramaka, Aluku, and Kwinti worshipped Nana the god of creation, the ancestors, and the serpent, sky, and bush spirits.

DUTCH CRIME & PUNISHMENT IN SURINAME

From Captain J. G. Stedman, *Narrative, of a Five Years' Expedition, Against the Revolted Negroes of Surinam, in Guiana . . . from the Year 1772, to 1777 . . . Volume I* (London, 1796).

"Not long ago . . . I saw a black man suspended alive from a gallows, by the ribs, between which, with a knife, was first made an incision, and then clinched an iron hook with a chain; in this manner he kept alive three days, hanging with his head and feet downwards . . . Another negro . . . I have seen quartered alive; who, after four strong horses were fastened to his legs and arms, and after having iron sprigs driven home underneath every one of his nails on hands and feet . . . As for old men being broken on the rack, and young women roasted alive chained to stakes, there can nothing be more common in this colony."

"The first object which attracted my compassion during a visit to a neighbouring estate, was a beautiful Samboe girl of about eighteen, tied up by both arms to a tree, as naked as she came into the world, and lacerated in such a shocking manner by the whips of two negro-drivers, that she was from her neck to her ancles literally dyed over with blood. It was after she had received two

hundred lashes that I perceived her, with her head hanging downwards, a most affecting spectacle. When, turning to the overseer,
I implored that . . . might be immediately unbound . . . but the short
answer which I obtained was, that to prevent all strangers from
interfering with his government, he had made an unalterable rule . . .
always to double the punishment, which he instantaneously began
to put in execution: I endeavoured to stop him, but in vain . . . Thus I
had no other remedy but to run to my boat, and leave the detest-
able monster, like a bird of prey, to enjoy his bloody feast, till he
was glutted."

About 250 of Suriname's 60,000 slaves ran away each year. In 1690,
the slaves there unleashed "a general terror" on the plantation of Immanuel
Machado on a tributary of the upper Commewijane River. In 1693, they
did the same at the plantation Providence, along the Suriname River. By
1749, 6,000 Maroons were on the run. Around 1,500 new freedom fighters
joined them every year. Between 1750 and 1759, fifteen revolts broke out.
The Maroon Wars would last two hundred years, until 1862.

To punish the rebels, the Dutch dispatched waves of warships from
Texel in Holland. Most troops ended up dying from disease, running
out of food and being forced to eat monkeys, marching around in circles
scared witless by nighttime drums, or ending up decapitated on wooden
spikes. This was the Maroons' revenge for their own people being hanged
on meat hooks, broken on wheels, sexually assaulted, roasted alive, and
beheaded on plantation estates. Following the British model in Jamaica,
the Dutch eventually sent a hundred soldiers up the Saramacca River in
October 1749, destroyed 415 Maroon houses, and only then set about
negotiating peace. In recognition of his people's newly won independence,
Captain Adoe, chief of the Seramica, was gifted a large cane with a silver
pommel engraved with heraldry of Suriname.

The Dutch-born Scottish soldier John Stedman wrote sympatheti-
cally about his experiences hunting the rebels from 1773 to 1777. In his
memoir, *Narrative of a Five Years Expedition Against the Revolted Negroes
of Suriname* (1796), he writes:

> *Some Afric chief will rise, who scorning chains,*
> *Racks, tortures, flames, excruciating pains,*
> *Will lead his injur'd friends to bloody fight,*
> *And in the flooded carnage take delight;*
> *Then dear repay us in some bloody war,*
> *And give us blood for blood, and fear for fear.*

On the shore of the Maroon village of Akalikondre, the air was thick with anticipation and nerves as various cultures, untrusting for centuries, were about to meet. Three men emerged out of the forest, cautious but relaxed. At center strolled the captain of the village wearing a camouflage hat and a vintage purple Chelsea Football Club shirt. A large silver cross swung protectively around his neck.

The groups stood apart and aloof, not quite sure how to act. The captain smiled gently and stared intently at the foreigners. Should he trust them or turn on his heels?

They all shook hands. The ice melted. The strangers made their way into the heart of the village. Chickens grubbed around the beaten earth in front of a wooden shuttered house painted sky blue with brick foundations, the same style of architecture used in Paramaribo centuries ago. Other homes were painted yellow or had fallen down. Tree roots slithered across the ground in a thirsty search for ground water. A curious youngster stuck her head out of the front door of a shack wearing a Sex Pistols T-shirt, still rebelling after all this time. Bare-chested Maroon men wondered what all the fuss was about.

The divers and villagers sat down stiffly in a circle. Before chatting, the village captain made a blessing and poured a libation of rum into the ground to appease the ancestors.

"Spirits in the ground we are begging you," he prayed. "Stand for us, small ones who are left behind today. Make the world see we are here. Here is where I grew up. Here is where I was raised. Here is where I was fed. I give you my thanks, Father. You are not here anymore, but your name is still here. Mothers, come and accept our gifts. Mother Bakalobi, mother Nali. Please accept this mother Lena, mother Mijeso, and mother Malo. Accept our gifts. Grandmothers and grandfathers, great-grandparents, great-great-grandparents. Please accept our gifts and stand with us. Yeeha."

MEETING A MAROON REBEL

A description of a rebel African slave in Suriname from Captain J. G. Stedman, *Narrative, of a Five Years' Expedition, Against the Revolted Negroes of Surinam, in Guiana . . . from the Year 1772, to 1777 . . . Volume II* (London, 1796).

"This rebel negro is armed with a firelock and a hatchet; his hair, though woolly, may be observed to be plaited close to his head, by way of distinction from the rangers . . . his beard is grown to a point . . . The principal dress of this man consists of a cotton sheet, negligently tied across his shoulders, which protects him from the weather, and serves him also to rest on . . . The rest of his dress is a camisa, tied around his loins like a handkerchief; his pouch, which is made of some animal's skin; a few cotton strings for ornament around his ancles and wrists; and a superstitious *obia* or amulet tied about his neck, in which he places all his confidence. The skull and ribs [also worn] are supposed to be the bones of his enemies, scattered upon the sandy Savannah."

The prayer finished, the captain drank to the bottom of the glass and poured the dregs of the rum over his hands, wrists, and face. The ancestors permeated into his very being.

Kramer watched, captivated. Diving With A Purpose would dive on ships where hundreds of Africans perished faceless, nameless, voiceless. Theirs was an ephemeral fate written in water. In Akalikondre he sensed overwhelming pride. The Maroons lived a meager existence, he noticed, but they were happy and proud because they fought and won their freedom. Kramer, searching for his own lost African ancestry, felt a warm affinity with these forest people.

Kinga had more immediate thoughts on her mind as she watched a village wife prepare a delicious-smelling communal meal over the fire, steaming the food under a banana leaf.

"This is cassava," Leo Balai explained. "We call it Tomtom. It is peanuts with rice."

The woman started frying up chicken and stock. Her friend watched on, clad in a black T-shirt emblazoned Smile.

The divers realized that even though the freedom fighters had struggled for liberty a couple of hundred years ago, the Maroons and their children, and the future generations, were fully aware of their tumultuous past. They remember and still teach their history.

Kramer beamed, joyful. He felt a release, uplifted that even in the midst of such historic brutality the Maroons' pride and the fighting spirit of African people won out.

Before serving up their chicken and rice, the village women dressed Alanna and Kinga in traditional blue, red, and white checked skirts and scarves. It was a mark of respect. They also knew this was hearty, messy food. The laughter spread. Leo Balai smiled on. The divers may not have uncovered the *Leusden* but they had come face-to-face with living descendants of Africans trafficked from Angola and Ghana, thousands of miles across the Middle Passage. These people had beaten the odds. Lived to tell the tale.

Looking around at the simple village existence so full of vitality, Alannah could not help but wonder. The African captives on the *Leusden* could have shared this life.

Kramer agreed and muttered out loud, "What if? What if they hadn't been murdered? What if they hadn't nailed down the hatches? If they hadn't sat on the hatches to make sure that they drowned and killed every last one of them. They could have saved themselves. It could have been another Maroon village."

As the new firm friends made their way back to the creek, back to their boat, Paramaribo, and the next slave wreck dive, Alannah asked the captain's right-hand man, "Baisha, do you know what country in Africa you're from or where everybody is from?"

The captain's translator explained how it is said that their tribe came mainly from Ghana. Alannah had heard about the mighty fort of Elmina on Ghana's Gold Coast, where hundreds of thousands of captive Africans were pushed through the Door of No Return, the African women raped in its loathsome chambers.

"Okay. How do they know?" Alannah checked.

"Their ancestors. From their grandparents. The other told the other and so on. As slaves they come from there," the captain told the divers.

"Baisha, have you ever been to Africa?" Kramer asked. He had not.

"Do you want to go?" Kramer followed up.

Baisha confirmed he did, smiling. He knew, though, it was a distant dream.

"If you did get the chance to go, would you call that home? Or is this home?" Alannah pressed.

"When we go there, I come back to here. This is my home," Baisha let everyone know.

The Americans, Dutchman, and Maroons all laughed. They came from different ends of the globe but shared the same roots, the same sense of identity, never forgetting the past. They were all survivors.

Down at the water's edge the rebels and divers shook hands and embraced. They would never forget this day. Hours ago, they never knew of one another's existence. Now by giving voice to their trauma, fighting for their rights and winning, everyone felt exuberant, inspired.

It was time to push on. More slave wrecks lay out there, their stories and the voices of the lost Africans needing raising from the deep.

Slaves to Profit

The transatlantic slave trade is not some irrelevant story that happened centuries ago, of no consequence to our sophisticated twenty-first-century ways. In Brazil, today, on the ruins of the Valongo's wharves, where hundreds of thousands of Africans arrived, their descendants hold religious ceremonies commemorating the deaths of Black senators. An ebo steer has been sacrificed on its paving stones and ritual charms spoken over the excavated finds to appease the ancestors clamoring for justice. A ritual of redemption poured flower-scented water over the quay and dedicated a large heart made of red roses spelling the word PEACE in white roses. The Valongo is now consecrated by law as sacred ground.

Still, Brazil is a country of great inequality, crime, and poverty. Slavery persisted until almost the twentieth century and its effects haunt the present. The city's Afro descendants have the least opportunities for studying, earn the lowest wages, and are forced to live in the most dangerous and degrading conditions. The roots of this social depression all started when their ancestors landed in Rio, were enslaved, and treated as inferior beings. The shackled stigma of inferiority is hard to break.

As sincerely as Rio de Janeiro has sought to give the city's Black community ownership of the Valongo past, across the Atlantic in Portugal, a planned memorial to honor the African dead under Lagos's mini-golf course is sunk in bureaucracy. Portugal is full of monuments to conquerors and explorers but is accused of trivializing its role in the slave trade. Slavery existed long before Portugal got involved, Lisbon pleads. Portugal, like Spain, is yet to apologize for the role it played.

The Maroons of Suriname are also still fighting. From Canada to Argentina, every nation in the Americas has given special legal protection to its Indigenous populations. The one exception is the Republic of Suriname, whose government insists the Maroons have no special rights. Their precious land can be ripped away whenever the government wants. Suriname shows no respect for history or the peace treaties signed with the Dutch in the 1760s that gave autonomy and territorial rights to the Maroons.

To the displaced Africans, the treaties are legitimate to this day. Suriname's government rejects them as out-of-date colonial trivia. The Maroons may be the majority population of the country's interior at 10 percent of Suriname's people, but they are treated as a minority taking up prime land for mining bauxite and gold, cutting timber, dam building, and ecotourism. To many city slickers, Suriname's Maroons are a Stone Age people without meaning to the modern world. Slavery was abolished in Suriname, in 1863. For the Maroons, the battle continues.

RATIONALIZATION

When a vessel arrived to conduct us away to the ship, it was a most horrible scene; there was nothing to be heard but rattling of chains, smacking of whips, and groans and cries of our fellow men . . .

—Quobna Ottobah Cugoano, *Thoughts and Sentiments on the Evil and Wicked Trade of the Slavery and Commerce of the Human Species* (1787)

THE OLDEST SLAVER

Mylor—Cornwall, England

The tragedy of the *Leusden* happened when the slave trade was in full gear. Now the investigation team was confronting the start of the trade 7,300 kilometers (about 4,500 miles) away in the English Channel. This is where the transatlantic slave trade first went truly global. London took over from Portugal and Spain in the late seventeenth century and built a monstrous machine in human trafficking. From the goods exported to buy Africans; to captains' contracts; the seizing of humans from Senegal, Gambia, Ghana, Benin, Nigeria, and Angola; and the handling of the ships that took them, nothing was left to chance. The slave trade was a meticulously planned evil.

Somewhere out there off southwest England, the earliest slave ship in the world had been discovered. This was a unique chance to get up close and personal with what the trade looked like in its early years. This would also be by far the team's most dangerous operation.

The sea calmly licked the stone harbor wall at Mylor in Cornwall, the first landfall for ships returning to England from Africa and the Caribbean. The early morning sky was crystal clear. It was going to be a fine autumnal day to dive. The English Channel is the opposite of the tropical calm of the Florida Keys, Diving With A Purpose's home base. More often than not, forbidding gray skies hung over churning waters.

In the later seventeenth century, England was the master of the slave trade. Between 1640 and 1807, 3.1 million Africans were shipped to the Caribbean plantations in English hulls. Around 400,000 died in the Middle Passage between Africa's Gold and Slave Coasts and the backbreaking plantations of Barbados and Jamaica. Together, England and Portugal were responsible for 70 percent of all Africans trafficked throughout colonial history. Britain, though, was the dominant player in eight of the thirteen decades from 1681 to 1807.

The shores of England were a launchpad for an inexplicable evil that jars the modern mind. Why did London "industrialize" the greatest enslavement history ever witnessed? How did its merchants manage the trade and what was life like for the enslaved? To make sense of unfathomable numbers and statistics, Diving With A Purpose—Kramer Wimberley, Alannah Vellacott, and Kinga Philipps, now joined by Joshua Williams—and helped by British specialist deep divers, Richard Stevenson and Kieran Hatton, would have to head seventy kilometers (around forty-three miles) offshore. And then somehow descend 110 meters to scrutinize a wreck codenamed Site 35F.

There was one major problem. No human had ever dived the wreck before. Only a handful of scientists had even locked eyes on its secrets using an unmanned remotely operated vehicle (ROV). Dr. Sean Kingsley, an English marine archaeologist, was one of the few. The team had come to Mylor to meet Sean, hear how the rare wreck came to light, what they might find, and to figure out how to crack the lost ship's secrets.

Hellbound

Looking out to sea toward a frightening ship lost beyond the sight of land, Dr. Kingsley pulled no punches. The project was ultra-dangerous. The risks were high, the rewards great.

From royal warships to floating treasure chests, French pirates and Nazi submarines on secret missions, the English Channel shatters dreams for kicks. It respects nobody, neither prince nor ship's cook. These Narrow Seas were Britain's communications highway centuries before planes, trains, automobiles, and the World Wide Web. From here fleets set out into the Atlantic in search of wealth, land, power, and people.

This highway to hell was invaded seven times every century over the last nine hundred years. Mostly the weather, not brilliant commanders and heavily armed warships, forced enemies into retreat. The brave few who did make landfall—Julius Caesar and the Roman Empire in 55 B.C.E. and Norman invaders from France in 1066—changed the course of history. Down the centuries, thirty-seven thousand ships sank off England's deadly waters.

Diving With A Purpose would need to head to a place where the mouth of the English Channel meets what captains called the Western Approaches. These are perilous seas: battered by wind and wave, beyond the sight of land, and deep. The team had better get a good night's sleep, Dr. Kingsley warned, because this was not just another dive. This was extreme marine archaeology.

The team learned how, in the late seventeenth century, half a day from returning to home base in London, the unidentified ship, now given the bland discovery name "35F," got into trouble. Its wooden walls were whipped by mountainous waves. Sails, rigging, and crew whistled overboard. The anchors were useless, manning the sails and resisting the wind pointless. After two years at sea, the crew was doomed.

This was not how it was supposed to end. The hard graft was over, the cargos bartered half a world away safely secured in the hold. In the last weeks, all the crew had dreamed about was how they would spend their hard-earned gains.

The end came suddenly. After months in tropical Caribbean waters, the patched-up hull was rotten, attacked by armies of shipworms, the silent assassins of the seas. Water poured through cracks between planks. Part of the cargo was slung over the side in a last-ditch effort to pay the devil for salvation. The carpenter and cook made a run for it, throwing themselves into the charging "white horses," white crested waves. They were never seen again.

The captain manned the helm till the bitter end. Then a colossal wave sucked him down into the abyss. With his final breath, he must have wondered if he should have done the right thing and unbolted the hatches leading below deck. His paymasters in London would have been disgusted by the very idea. The captain must have pushed the thought to the back of his exhausted mind. Rattling chains and the screams of the few enslaved heading to serve Britain were probably the last sounds the slave trader heard.

Narrow Seas

The world's oldest slave ship was found by a high-tech yellow robot called Zeus, an intrepid new generation of deep-sea explorer designed to beat the odds. The seven-ton robot runs on fiber optics and electricity, not oxygen, and is the eyes and hands of archaeologists where it is too deep to dive. The most sophisticated archaeologically tooled robot in the world could boldly swim through high waves and strong currents to places no human had gone before and stay there as long as needed.

Site 35F came to light by chance during the world's biggest deep-sea sunken search run by Odyssey Marine Exploration. Somewhere out there between England and France was dazzling Spanish, French, and English treasure. The Americans were determined to hunt it down. They had hit pay dirt before. For example, they had recovered 51,000 gold and silver coins from the Civil War–era shipwreck of the SS *Republic*.

Off the coast of Gibraltar they also discovered the *Nuestra Señora de las Mercedes,* a Spanish ship blown up by the Royal Navy in 1804, whose treasure of 14.5 tons of silver coins was said to be worth a cool $500 million today. The Odyssey boys flew the booty to Tampa to claim it in the courts, but the bet backfired. When the Spanish government moved in on the find, Odyssey was forced to hand it back to Madrid. A few years later they netted 109 tons of silver ingots, 4,700 meters deep off southwest Ireland, from the British India steamship the SS *Gairsoppa*. This time they got to keep it.

Site 35F was a double crime scene. First, it was an ancient echo of the slave trade. Secondly, it had been ransacked in the modern day. When the wreck was first discovered by Odyssey, side-scan sonar images showed disturbing lines running through its heart. Mega-trawlers raking the seabed for shellfish had crushed the delicate cultural remains. Site 35F had been put through a shredder. History's hard drive had been wiped to put fish and chips on dinner tables.

WRECK SITE 35F

- Royal African Company merchant ship
- London to Ghana, Caribbean, and England
- Keel 26.1 meters long, 600 tons capacity, and crew of 70 (?)
- 48 iron cannons for protection and sale
- Sunk *ca.* 1672–1685, Western Approaches to England
- Depth 110 meters
- Cargo: elephant tusks, manilla copper bracelets, stacks of copper basins, sugar, slaves, and gold (?)
- Small finds: English wine bottles, tobacco pipe, ceramics, wooden folding ruler, cannonballs, galley bricks, lead hull sheeting, and concreted iron rigging

Site 35F is not the *Titanic*. It does not stand proudly above the seabed defying time. It has been flattened into a low mound. No more than forty centimeters of its crushed decks are left today. Enough survives to reconstruct the old ship, its stern to the northeast, the bow to the southwest. Underwater surveys had shown that 35F was once a force to be reckoned with. The sea floor around it is littered with forty-eight iron cannons, bits and pieces of ceramic pots, wine bottles, tobacco pipes, a pile of copper basins, elephant tusks, and round copper bracelets used as currency in Africa.

Elephant tusks and copper "manilla" bracelets are extremely rare among the world's three million shipwrecks. They are monstrous artifacts exclusively used in the African slave trade that make the hairs on the back of explorers' necks stand up—immortal memories of Europe's trade in ivory, gold, and humans. There was no doubt about it, Site 35F stank of guilt. But could they prove that it was a slave ship and, if they could, would they be able to identify its nationality and owners? The detective work began in earnest.

The Odyssey team and Dr. Kingsley realized this was a big vessel, perhaps six hundred tons, and manned by a crew of around seventy. Here and there, a few wooden planks were spotted with signs they had been patched up with a double layer of wood. This naval technique, known as "furring," was a kind of protection used in tropical waters to slow down shipworms feasting on hulls. Furring was a European method for ships that sailed in warm tropical waters. This ship had undoubtedly worked the Americas before the early eighteenth century. If it was a slave ship, it would be the earliest ever identified. If it was English, it would have belonged to the Royal African Company, a London trading company set up in 1672 by the royal family. The company gave itself a national monopoly over the slave trade for almost two decades.

RED GOLD

Legend has it that manilla bracelets were first made in West Africa from copper bolts salvaged from wrecked ships. They were manufactured by the millions but are rare finds on just a few wrecks off France, Spain, England, Bermuda, Cape Verde, and Ghana.

The scale of the manilla trade was colossal. By 1635 up to 763 tons of copper were being shipped to West Africa a year in Dutch, English, and French ships. Portugal's copper was mainly mined in Flanders (modern Belgium), but was also bought in Venice and Morocco. At the end of the fifteenth century, 80 percent of the manillas shipped out of Lisbon—seventy-one thousand bracelets—went to the fort of Elmina in Ghana.

Traders started looking for ways to make manillas more cheaply and boost profits. In the 1720s, Robert Morris of London thinned the copper by mixing every ton with half a ton of lead. The Cheadle company in Greenfield, Warrington, the Forest Copper Works in Swansea, and Thomas Williams's Holywell Works in Flintshire soon jumped on the bandwagon. When Bristol turned into the leading port for the English slave trade in the 1710s, Thomas Williams became known as the Copper King.

How many manillas were manufactured by Europe to buy Africa's elephants, gold, and people is not recorded. The numbers were staggering. In 1949, when authorities forced Nigeria to move to a monetary economy after World War II—not one based on cowrie shells and copper bars—32.5 million manillas were handed over.

In the early surveys of the site, nine tusks, each up to 1.4 meters long and weighing twenty-four kilograms (over fifty pounds), were identified scattered over the bows, a fraction of the cargo once rounded up in West Africa. No doubt the rest had been harvested in fishermen's nets, now scattered to the four winds. Over a quarter of a million tusks left West Africa, mostly in English and Dutch holds, between 1699 and 1725. At its peak, sixty-one tons reached London every year.

Underwater, bright green bracelets shone forth from the seabed among the sand and gravel as if they were desperate not to be forgotten by the future. Each bracelet measured around 9 x 7 centimeters and weighed up to 140 grams (about five ounces). They were tiny finds with a huge impact. Slave traders called them manillas, from the Latin word *manus* (hand) or *monilia* (necklace or neckring).

Manillas were a sinister cog in a machine designed to get West Africa addicted to Western goods. European merchants had noticed how African women wore their money on their arms and legs in the form of copper bracelets. At market, they used this currency to buy and sell. By imitating their design, the West settled on a cheap way to get Africa to part with its brothers and sisters. Manillas made in Europe were specially designed as a currency to buy gold, elephant tusks, and humans.

MANILLAS IN AFRICA

Since manillas became the currency of trade, West Africans were very particular about their quality. Dr. Dapper's *Description de l'Afrique (Description of Africa)* showed in 1668 how, "Along the river of Kalbaria [Calabar, Nigeria] the white races . . . trade with the inhabitants, and in exchange for slaves offer rough grey copper armlets, which must be oblong with a rounded curve and very well made, since the natives are very particular on these points and frequently will reject two or three hundred out of one barrel . . . the armlets brought there by white men, which they call Bochie, are used solely for money."

What could a manilla bracelet get you? Portuguese merchants at Calabar in Nigeria could buy an African for eight to ten copper manillas in 1505. By 1517, a plantation slave cost fifty-seven manillas. An ounce of gold cost eighty manillas in 1556. In 1681, around the time when 35F sank off the Western Approaches, the Royal African Company merchant John Thorne was buying one slave for two hundred bracelets.

Company ships headed to Africa with thousands of "manilloes black" and "manilloes bright" made of copper and brass. The Royal African Company's copper came from Sweden, Germany, Hungary, and Morocco. At first, in 1673, one ton of manillas was used to test the waters in Africa. Then the floodgates opened. By 1700, a colossal forty-six tons had reached the Gold Coast.

35F's nationality is a crucial question. The glass wine bottles on the wreck looked like the goods made in John Baker's glasshouse in London's Vauxhall until it was demolished in 1706. But bottles like this were also made in Holland and France. The smoking gun turned out to be a lucky strike. A sliver of rectangular wood preserved by pure fortune, etched all over with marks, letters, and numbers, was one half of a two-foot wooden folding ruler. Rulers like this were kept handy in carpenters' chests to work out mathematical areas and volumes of timber to be sawn into ship-building parts. It worked like a slide rule with a pair of dividers. Folding rulers are rarer than hen's teeth and this was the oldest "pocket calculator" found underwater. The best brains dated it to the 1670s or 1680s.

It was a tiny detail in the ruler that in the end gave away the ship's nationality. Dutch, German, and French carpenters all used slightly different units of measurement. 35F's folding ruler was designed using the inch measuring 2.54 centimeters. Only one nation stubbornly preferred this formula: England.

The final fragment of the puzzle slotted into place. 35F was an English merchantman returning from a trading voyage to West Africa and the Caribbean, only to end up decimated by a storm half a day from home, probably between 1672 and 1685.

The forensics pointed to an inescapable reality. When it sank, the ship was in the service of one of the darkest merchant monopolies English history witnessed: the Royal African Company, run by the king's brother, James, the Duke of York. The company was in the business of buying massive amounts of gold, elephant tusks, and captives all along the coast of West Africa. At the height of the trade a ship left London, Bristol, or Liverpool to hunt for slaves every second day.

BIRMINGHAM MANILLAS

W. J. Davis, *A Short History of the Brass Trade* (1892): "it will perhaps not be uninteresting to mention that many ton of Manilla money are annually cast in Birmingham. This is a species of ring money used in Africa and on Spanish settlements in Calabar. It was first made of alloy of copper and lead, and hardened with arsenic. Nearly thirty years ago the black mint master of the African tribe visited Birmingham to inspect the pieces. It is said that the degree of rank in this tribe is determined solely by the possession of these articles: those having the most being the wealthy members, and, as a consequence, have proportionate sway. Livingstone, Stanley, and other travellers tell us, that when about to penetrate into the interior of the dark continent, they had to provide themselves with cloth, beads, looking glasses, and brass wire, to be used as a medium of exchange with the natives, as much as would make good loads for 40 or 50 natives to carry. These things afterwards served the double purpose of personal finery and money. Orders for wire for this purpose amount to many tons a year. Rings or 'Bangles' made of thick solid wire, or tube, or even cast, are also made here, and sent in large consignments for the adornment of African swells and belles. One order amounted to 20,000 dozen of rings, 3½ inches in diameter, weighing 23 tons."

Mission Impossible

Investigating 35F would be a dangerous challenge for Diving With A Purpose. It was a gamble. Dr. Kingsley could not even guarantee anything of the ship survived. The wreck had not been looked at in years. It

was 50/50 that fishing trawlers had bulldozed its remains so catastrophi-
cally that nothing was left to bear witness to the thousands of English
slave voyages that once crossed the Western Approaches.

"No one has put eyes on this wreck for ten years now," Dr. Kingsley
told the team. "We don't even know if it still exists. So your mission is
to get out there, try and rediscover the site and see what other bits of
information we can extract to add to our story."

"And by the way," the scientist who would not be going offshore
warned, "when there is a storm here, it's the perfect storm."

The team was left to chew over the risks ahead. The odds were stacked
against them. They needed the notorious British weather to behave
for just one October day. Not even English warships went out in this
weather. If you were caught on the high seas in October, you got what
you deserved, King George II's commanders used to say. This was perfect
storm time of year.

With their mission impossible set, the nervous team pored over sea
charts with Sacha Hall, who would lead the dive boat in search of 35F.
Sacha had seen it all in these waters. He pointed out on a map how the
wreck lay in a danger zone where the wide Atlantic tightens into a funnel
between the two narrow arms of England and France. It was a natural choke
point. Here the waves grow in height and the seas get more ferocious.

"To dive the site, the conditions have to be good, calm, perfect, and
flat," Sacha shrugged. "For all those factors to come together, we'll need
a small window of opportunity."

The team would need a minor miracle. The next stop was the middle
of nowhere, the cruel Narrow Approaches, to explore what African voices
could be brought back to life from a shipwrecked grave.

The team felt a heavy burden of responsibility.

KINGDOM OF LOANGO

Today, most of the natural and cultural landscapes where Europe's traders bartered and trafficked Africans would be unrecognizable to a time traveler from the seventeenth, eighteenth, or nineteenth century. Concrete urban jungles have replaced sprawling forests. Traditional villages built of wooden poles and mud walls have left no traces for archaeologists to explore. The African kingdoms' art was hoovered up by pith-helmeted English, French, German, and Austrian explorers. One unique area, though, retains a feel of times gone by, an opportunity to visualize–and rationalize–the landscapes and cultures from where the trafficked millions were dispossessed.

The kingdom of Loango is a rare exception. Stretching from Cape Lopez in the north to the Congo River in the south, the 460-mile coast now spanning Gabon, Angola, and the Democratic Republic of the Congo was dragged into the transatlantic slave trade around 1660. Unlike much of West Africa, where heavy industry has stripped the forests bare, a thin slice of times past endures. Gabon in particular, at 88 percent rainforest, is the second most forested country on the planet. Miles of dense trees run deep inland and down to the coast.

Gabon also remains a rare sanctuary for over 60 percent of Africa's forest elephants. The snaking Ogooue River in Loango National Park, flanked by forbidding dense forest, once offered a convenient way to paddle upriver to tribal villages. Equatorial Guinea and Cameroon lie to the north and the Democratic Republic of the Congo runs to the east. The Ogooue River drains the whole of Gabon down to a wide estuary before pouring out into the mighty Atlantic Ocean. Green savannah and sandy shores replace haunted forests. It is not hard to sense the slave trade and imagine wooden slave ships bobbing menacingly close to shore. For centuries, enchained Africans and tusks, sawn off butchered elephants, were trafficked down these river highways to hell.

Even today, keeping elephants free to roam in their natural habitat has to be closely protected by eco-guards, who put their bodies on the line fighting poachers. The war that slaughtered millions of these gentle beasts since the sixteenth century is still raging. Gun battles between rangers and poachers break out every month, just like in the slave days. Now, however, they are feeding a demand mostly driven by East and Southeast Asia, where ivory is regarded as an amulet and a status symbol. Selling ivory may be illegal, but it still brings in $2,000 a kilogram on the black market.

It was here that the first transatlantic slaving voyage departed the Congo River, the southern boundary of the Loango Coast, with a captive cargo in 1514. The Portuguese ship picked up 237 Africans, mostly destined for Vigo in Spain; 69 died in the sea crossing. In centuries gone by, people were marched for three months from the interior down to the slave ships, while others were paddled down in canoes. Along with humans, forty kilograms (about eighty-eight pounds) of tusks and ebony wood were dragged to the shore. Either way, the Atlantic was the end of the line.

In the slave trade days, this historic landscape was the heart of the kingdom of Loango, which by the late eighteenth century was the back-drop to half of all slave transports from West Africa. Europe's super-powers prized open trade routes deep inland to exploit the rainforest's riches, including African men, women, and children.

Portuguese traders at first bought palm cloth, redwood, ivory, ele-phant tails, and copper, which was used to barter for slaves in Angola. In exchange, they introduced cloth, iron goods, alcohol, guns, ammunition, and beads into the region. The trade in humans took off in Dutch holds in 1651, followed by British dominance between 1721 and 1740, the French until 1790, the Portuguese from 1811 to 1850, and finally the Americans for the last thirteen years of the trade. At least 475,000 slaves entered the transatlantic slave trade through the ports of the Loango Coast between 1660 and 1810, and another 1.3 million from 1811 to 1867.

Slave traders expected to spend four months in Africa securing their human cargo. Corralling them onboard ship took one and a half months. The cost of slaves varied between the equivalent of £17.5 and £26.9 between 1681 and 1750. The value of a Loango Coast slave peaked at £77.9 around 1790.

Most of the prisoners were channeled through the Valley of the Slaves to be shipped out of Africa by way of the Iguela Lagoon, eighty-five achingly beautiful square miles studded with tiny islands. Before the captives were shipped and shackled for the Americas, they were given a last supper. After all, it was in the traders' best interests to keep the slaves functioning and healthy. Strong slaves meant bigger profits.

In the Iguela Lagoon European merchants could keep their captives well fed and cut costs at the same time. In these tranquil bays the archaeologist Dr. Richard Oslisly recently turned up traces of the mind-boggling scale of slave trafficking in millions of discarded oyster shells. The lagoon has always been rich in nutritional oysters. Over time the last suppers fed to the enslaved built up a whole island whose foundations were made up solely of oysters—two and a half thousand acres of shells piled up to four meters high. Each discarded shell symbolizes the death of hope.

AMERICAN SLAVERS ON THE CONGO

A March 2, 1860, description of American slavers on the coast of Congo in the *New York Times* described how "they sail boldly in, anchor, and in two or three hours are filled with negroes, who are carried off to them in canoes. The refractory ones are clapped in irons, or made drunk with rum; and in this stupefied condition they are carried aboard, stowed in a sitting posture, with the knees drawn up so closely that they can scarcely breathe, much less move.

"Now their sufferings become dreadful—horrible; indeed, human language is incapable of describing, or imagination of sketching even the faint outline of a dimly floating fancy of what their condition is—homesick, seasick, half starved, naked, crying for air, for water, the strong killing the weak or dying in order to make room, the hold becomes a perfect charnel house of death and misery—a misery and anguish only conceivable by those who have endured it."

For most of the enchained Africans seized deep in the forests, this was the first time they saw the ocean, let alone those strange floating trees called ships. Families were torn apart and cultures destroyed for 351 long years until 1865 when the *Cicerón*, a Liverpool steamship, sailed from Cadiz to the Congo River and took a last group of enslaved Africans.

What were conditions like for the dispossessed forced to sail the Middle Passage? In 1667, Capuchin priest Dionigi de Carli left behind a rare early account after boarding a Portuguese ship loaded at Luanda in modern Angola on the Loango Coast. On a fifty-day voyage to Brazil, he matter-of-factly reported in his *Curious and Exact Account of a Voyage to Congo*, how

> The Ship I went onboard . . . was loaded with Elephants Teeth and Slaves, to the number of 680 Men, Women, and Children. It was a pitiful sight to behold, how all these People were bestow'd. The men were standing in the Hold, fastned one to another by Stakes, for fear they should rise and kill the Whites. The Women were between the Decks, and those that were with Child in the great Cabin, the Children in the steeridg, press'd together like Herrings in a Barrel, which caus'd an intolerable heat and stench.

Where the Ogooue River meets the Atlantic Ocean, the light changes from the somber overcast darkness of the forests to a glaring yellow horizon shimmering off the water. The enormity of the world opens up. The big slave ships stood at anchor awaiting their human cargos. From an isolated shore, feared even by Europeans for its mighty surf and underwater earthquakes, a future in chains and sleepless days breaking your back in the fields was only weeks away. The moment the inland Africans saw the ships for the first time, all hope ran out and was replaced by absolute terror.

Two hundred years ago, this tropical paradise was hell on earth. Next stop was Brazil, Cuba, the United States, England, or the bottom of the ocean.

OUT OF AFRICA

Sasha's *Severn Sea* research ship plowed through the English Channel. The team was not bursting with adrenalin and excitement like on most wreck dives, but was silent, deep in reflection. They were sailing treacherous waves in search of the world's most perilous trade. When you think about the slave trade, the horrors can be imagined but kept at arm's length. Physically seeing man's shame is raw, emotional.

Each of the Diving With A Purpose dive team was battling their own personal journey. Alannah Vellacott's father was British, but her mother came from the Bahamas, a descendant of slaves trafficked from Africa. She was straddling two conflicting ancestry lines, trying to make sense of who she was.

There was plenty of time to prepare for whatever lay below. The wreck was marooned five hours offshore. On the way out the team caught up on the backstory of the Royal African Company and how one of its ships ended up lost half a day from home.

Black London

35F began its final voyage in London, the headquarters of the Royal African Company. African House had pride of place between Fenchurch and Leadenhall Street, a few minutes' walk north of the River Thames. Company ships docked between the awe-inspiring majesty of the Tower of London and London Bridge. Here the captain of 35F anchored among a forest of ships' masts and hurried past the king's Customs House to pick up his sailing instructions from the lords of the Royal African Company.

By the 1670s Black slaves were an exotic but common sight on London's streets from the royal court to private houses. Most people had no clue where they came from. They were either Black-skinned, what the Portuguese called *negro* (from the Latin word for black), or the color of moors (from the dark brown fields of Europe). Londoners found it easier to lazily call all captive Africans "blackamores."

Africans served in a range of positions, from a royal trumpeter to a sea diver, laundresses, soldiers, needle makers, and goldsmiths. Africans were so fashionable in London by 1680 that it was callously said a lady of fashion was almost obliged to "hath two necessary implements about her; a blackamore and her dog."

Absolutely nothing is known about where these displaced peoples were born, their fears and hopes. Only a few of their Western names survive. The odd medical record remembers how "Polonia the blackmor maid at Mr Peirs" suffered from "a fever . . . faint heart full of melancholy" in 1597. "Nicholas a Negro of unknown parents . . . at the age of 3 yeares or thereabouts" was baptized in St. Margaret's Westminster in 1619, while "Anthony, a poore ould Negro aged 105 yeares" died in Hackney in 1630. "Black Lucy" was forced from slavery into prostitution. What these people's parents called their children when they were born has vanished into thin air.

The architect of Black London and the slaves sent to backbreaking work cultivating the sugar and tobacco plantations in the Caribbean was the Royal African Company. The company had the kind of connections you did not mess with. Through its governor and chief backer, James, Duke of York, and future king of England, it enjoyed a cartel-like monopoly. King Charles II gave the company his royal approval on September 27, 1672. The Duke of York's men were bulletproof in its first three decades. Its charter gave it the exclusive trade rights to five thousand miles of the West coast of Africa from Morocco to the Cape of Good Hope in South Africa. Never mind that the same land occupied for millennia by Indigenous communities was never theirs to give away. The company's aim was to export cheap trifles in exchange for gold, elephants' tusks, wax, wood used for dyeing textiles, and humans, and maximize profits.

ROYAL AFRICAN COMPANY: TRUTH IN NUMBERS

Between 1672 and 1690, the widest dates when the Site 35F ship sailed, the Royal African Company made 279 voyages to West Africa. The company took most Africans in these years in Whydah (67 voyages), Calabar (southeast Nigeria, 40), West Central Africa and St. Helena (35), Gambia (24), New Calabar (eastern Nigeria, 22), the Gold Coast (22), the Bight of Biafra, and Gulf of Guinea Islands (10).

In this period the company signed charter contracts for the purchase of 65,411 Africans. In the end, 67,723 Africans were taken (3.5 percent more than chartered). Twenty-one percent died crossing the Middle Passage. The main Caribbean and American ports where the enslaved were disembarked from Company ships were Barbados (96 voyages), Jamaica (93), Nevis (36), Virginia (11), and Antigua (8).

The Site 35F trader could be any one of fifty-five ships documented in the company's archives as wrecked or fate unknown. Just two are listed as specifically "wrecked" or "destroyed," the *Providence* of 1679 and the *Lindsey* of 1686.

The *Providence*, Theodore Tyler captain, sailed from London to West Central Africa. The crew started buying Africans on May 23, 1679, and left for Jamaica on August 16, 1679. The ship was chartered to take 330 Africans, but shipped 223, including 24 women. Forty-three people died in the crossing.

The *Lindsey*, James Butler captain, sailed from London for West Central Africa on October 22, 1685. Five hundred captives were chartered for shipment to Barbados; 528 were eventually taken. On November 23, 1686, 458 reached the plantations, and 70 died en route.

Whether Site 35F is the *Providence* or the *Lindsey* may never be known. The archaeological evidence has been too heavily destroyed by fishing trawlers.

Before heading for West Africa, company ships picked up a department store of goods in London's African House to sell: everything from

British cloth and Swedish and German iron and copper to French brandy and glass beads sourced in Holland and Venice. Muskets and pistols were eagerly snapped up by West African rulers to get an edge fighting neighboring kingdoms.

Gold bartered mainly in modern Ghana was shipped to the Royal Mint in London, where it was turned into guinea coins stamped with the logo of the Royal African Company, an elephant with a castle on its back, symbols of profit and power. Around 548,000 gold guineas were cast from African gold between 1673 and 1713. Tusks were more expensive than humans and were mostly bought in Gambia and today's Ivory Coast between Ghana and Liberia. About 215 tons were imported into London every decade.

When creaking hulls could take no more enslaved Africans, elephant tusks, and gold, crews set out across the loathsome Middle Passage on the second leg of the triangular trade between West Africa and the Caribbean. Sometimes the whole proceeds from slave sales were paid in bills of exchange, a kind of check, stuffed into a wallet. Sailing home weighed down by unsold goods or just ballast was bad business, though, which most skippers tried to avoid. Barbados, Jamaica, and Nevis were famous for that rapturous, exotic, mouth-watering commodity—sugar. In 1677 alone, forty-three Royal African Company ships carried Caribbean sugar to London, each stocked with thirty-two tons of white crystals.

Sugar and humans' sweet tooth drove the transatlantic trade's engine from the very start. All in all, the Royal African Company sent over five hundred ships to West Africa between 1672 and 1713, from small boats of less than fifty tons to mega-traders of over four hundred tons.

The Middle of Nowhere

Five hours after setting out, the research ship *Severn Sea* finally reached the Site 35F wreck site. The research ship shut down its engines, a tiny speck beyond the view of England or France in the middle of nowhere. The team moved like clockwork. The target's coordinates were roughly known from Odyssey's previous robotic investigation, but hunting down this needle in a soggy haystack would still take time. And time was precious and expensive on a large boat far out to sea, where the weather window could change in an instant.

Even the planet's most skilled divers can spend no more than thirty minutes at a depth of 110 meters, so a Cougar XT remotely operated vehicle would be sent to try and locate the old ship. The remote-controlled robot was equipped with cameras, sonar, and sensors to let the crew scrutinize the seabed. Live images would be fed up to the research ship's control room from where the robot would be flown using a joystick. ROVs are the world's most expensive video games.

Six divers crowded around the television screen in breathless antici-pation as the ROV ended its five-minute commute down to the seabed. Plumes of algae cascaded sideways through the water column. Staring at the deep for too long made you dizzy. Slowly the team's eyes adjusted to the marine environment. A flat seabed was cut by low sand ripples, interrupted by the odd rock, crab, and conger eel.

There was little life down there and no sign of ancient wreckage. The ROV systematically searched the abyss. Time passed and the team shrugged. Maybe the entire wreck had been lost to fishing trawlers. Or was it all covered up by sand? Today, it seemed, was not going to be the day.

When hope was fading, a bright spot lit up the ROV's sonar. Any-thing bright-colored was material sticking up above the seabed. The next few minutes would tell whether it was natural geology or cultural remains.

The bright spots suddenly turned into lines, and the sonar shined like a Christmas tree. The sides were too straight to be made by Mother Nature. Then, on the live video stream, a cannon appeared out of the gloom, and then more, coated in thick concretion formed around the rusted iron submerged for so long.

The ROV headed for a closer look, all eyes glued to the screen. This was what Diving With A Purpose had crossed the Atlantic to see. The cascabels from the back of the guns, where fuses were lit to hurl iron cannonballs at enemy decks, could be clearly traced. The seabed was a forest of iron guns. This was no random artillery jettisoned by a passing warship. No doubt about it, X marked the spot of an historic wreck.

The ROV hovered over the wooden hull, cannonballs and concretions containing who knew what. Then a curved length of something made of bone snapped into focus, almost completely camouflaged on the seabed. Seaweed growing off its back danced in the current. The object looked out of place, not part of the natural habitat. The divers gasped when its true nature became clear. Far from home, it was a tusk from an elephant that once roamed free in the wilds of West Africa. A graceful creature murdered in the slave trade cycle to feed England with gold, African captives, and ivory.

The tusk's jagged ends were sharp, not waterworn. It had been freshly snapped off, desecrated by passing fishing trawlers. Elephant teeth were exactly what Royal African Company slave ships carried as homebound cargo. This living memory was once stored next to African captives in the wooden hull, perhaps the very ancestors of the team captivated by the images beamed up from the deep. The divers were relieved to have rediscovered the wreck. They had met the ancestors. At the same time, they were angry and confused.

Time was precious and emotions had to be set aside to deal with practicalities here and now. Should the tusk be recovered or left untouched as a silent gravestone memorializing human history's darkest times? So little survives of Site 35F. Its very existence is endangered, like the people the Royal African Company once trafficked and the slaughtered elephants whose teeth were ripped out by the millions. The suffering seems never to end.

The team was united about the right way ahead. "Bringing this tusk up is going to be raising the voices of people who didn't have a voice," Alannah stressed. "That tusk was worth maybe hundreds of lives of slaves. It's giving people like you and me an artifact to connect to. That tusk is a symbol of the pillaging of Africa. It can help a lot of people identify with that."

"Absolutely, we should do it," Kinga Philipps agreed. The question was how to lift it in the safest way? Recovering the tusk was going to be a major hurdle. For reasons that make little sense, English marine law forbids mechanical devices like ROV robots from touching cultural artifacts underwater. Which meant there was only one way to save it. If Diving With A Purpose wanted the tusk, they would have to go down and get it.

Diving so deep is a massive risk. Qualified tech divers like Kramer Wimberley can get down to forty meters. Site 35F was almost three times deeper. Richard Stevenson, the project's senior diver, was one of few people in the world to have mastered the art. Rich is daring but calculating. He sucked in the salty sea air to collect his thoughts and told the team, "It is deep but there is a way we can do it safely with rebreathers and mixed gases. For that, everything needs to be aligned perfectly. We need perfect conditions, good dive planning, and a great support team."

The group would never get this chance again. It was now or never. As Site 35F decays and eventually vanishes, the preservation of this crucial piece of history relied on the team's decision right now.

Kinga summed up the team's feelings. "Our options are either tell the story or walk away. And unless we bring something up, we're only really telling a portion of the story." The friends nodded in agreement.

"So, from what I'm hearing, we're going for it," Kramer smiled.

The deep dive for the voices of the African slave trade was a go. The *Severn Sea* was headed back to shore to gear up and leave nothing to chance. The divers had locked eyes on the scene of the crime, a ship like the thousands on which millions of African men, women, and children were stacked like cattle and sold into captivity. How had they ended up caught, enslaved, and sold? What experiences did ships like 35F have in West Africa and how were such unthinkable numbers seized?

35F was the earliest Royal African Company slave trader ever discovered, maybe the earliest slave ship in the world. Diving With A Purpose planned to plant a flag on the dark side of the ocean. They were sending the first human being down to explore its decks.

ABOVE: The Dutch slaving headquarters of Fort Zeelandia at Paramaribo in Suriname. By Gerard Voorduin and Jacob Eduard van Heemskerck van Beest, 1860–1862. *From Creative Commons.* BELOW: In Paramaribo, Suriname, Diving With A Purpose discuss, with Dr. Leo Balai and Prof. Jerzy Gawronski, the Dutch West Indies Company slave ship the *Leusden.* The ship sank in 1738. Six hundred sixty-four enslaved Africans were drowned when they were locked into the hold by the European crew.

ABOVE: Prof. Elena Moran and Simcha Jacobovici examine photos of the remains of enslaved Africans found in a mass grave in Lagos, Portugal, where the African slave trade began in the sixteenth century. A mini-golf course was built over the excavated cemetery. BELOW: Kramer Wimberley diving in the murky waters of Tiger Bank at the mouth of the Marowijne River, Suriname, in search of the *Leusden* shipwreck.

From the mid-sixteenth century onward, millions of enslaved were shipped to sugar plantations in Recife, Brazil, to cut sugarcane.

ABOVE: Ruins of the Valongo wharf in Rio de Janeiro where millions of enslaved Africans were landed in Brazil. *From Creative Commons.* BELOW: Traveling to an abandoned plantation in Suriname.

ABOVE: In the jungle with Dr. Leo Balai, exploring the rusting remains of an abandoned Dutch colonial sugar factory, once manned by enslaved Africans in Suriname. BELOW: Alannah Vellacott hears about their heritage from Captain Akoloi Kandre in a Maroon village in Suriname. These people's ancestors were runaway slaves who fought for and won their freedom in the eighteenth century.

ABOVE: The dive team watching the ROV robot locate the late seventeenth-century Site 35F wreck of a Royal African Company ship in the English Channel. BELOW: Divers in the English Channel. From left to right: Richard Stevenson, Kieran Hatton, Alannah Vellacott, Kinga Philipps, and Kramer Wimberley.

ABOVE: Elephant tusks wedged under an iron cannon on the Site 35F wreck, Western Approaches to England. BELOW: Copper manilla bracelets from the Site 35F wreck, Western Approaches. *Both images from Seascape Artifact Exhibits Inc.*

ABOVE: Elmina Castle on Ghana's Gold Coast. Over half of all Africans trafficked in the transatlantic trade passed through this fort and were held in its dungeons. BELOW: Diver Kramer Wimberley holds an elephant tusk recovered from the 110 meter-deep Site 35F wreck. During the slave trade, ivory was worth more than a trafficked African.

ABOVE: Bust of Kazoola in Africatown, Alabama. He was the last survivor of the *Clotilda*, the last slave ship to land on US soil in 1860. *From Creative Commons/Amy Walker.* BELOW: Mural of the slave ship the *Clotilda* in Mobile, Alabama. *From the Alabama Historical Commission and Alabama Tourism Department.*

Grammy Award–winning musician, Rhiannon Giddens, performs a song at the Kazoola Club in Mobile, Alabama. The banjo originated as an African, not Western, instrument.

ABOVE: Young Bribri divers get ready to dive the *Fredericus Quartus* and the *Christianus Quintus*, two Danish slave ships that went down in 1710, off the coast of Costa Rica. Some of the divers may be descended from the 751 enslaved Africans who made it to shore. BELOW: Youth diver Esteban Gallo preparing to dive the *Fredericus Quartus* and the *Christianus Quintus* with other Bribri divers.

ABOVE: Discovering Danish yellow brick ballast from the *Fredericus Quartus* and the *Christianus Quintus*, Cahuita National Park, Costa Rica. BELOW: Chef Matthew Raiford picks organic herbs at his farm on Jekyll Island, Georgia. In 1858, the *Wanderer*, the second to last slave ship to arrive in America, landed at Jekyll Island. Enslaved Africans brought their food traditions and culture with them.

ABOVE: The DWP dive team searches and records the galley area of the *Niagara* steamship, wrecked in Lake Michigan in 1856. As part of the Underground Railroad, runaways from the American South, masquerading as staff, made their way to freedom in Canada on the *Niagara*. BELOW: The Fisk Jubilee Singers perform the encoded slave resistance song "Wade in the Water" in the Fisk Memorial Chapel in Nashville.

ABOVE: Kinga Philipps in the bell tower in Saint John's Church in Cleveland, Ohio, where runaway slaves hid along the Underground Railroad before "freedom boats" took them on the last dangerous leg to Canada. BELOW: *Empire Sandy* is a topsail schooner similar to the *Home*, a freedom boat involved in the Underground Railroad, and identified at the bottom of Lake Michigan.

ABOVE: The wreck of the *Home* schooner in Lake Michigan, commanded by Underground Railroad abolitionist Captain James Nugent. It sunk in 1858. It is the first boat positively identified as a "freedom boat" that repeatedly smuggled African Americans to freedom. BELOW: Divers taking a reggae break while diving the pirate city at Port Royal, Jamaica.

ABOVE: Preparing to use magnetometers to search for remains of the slave ship the *London*, washed ashore in Rapparee Cove, Ilfracombe, in 1796. BELOW: Heading offshore to search for the wreck of the *London* at Ilfracombe, UK.

DESCRIPTION OF A SLAVE SHIP.

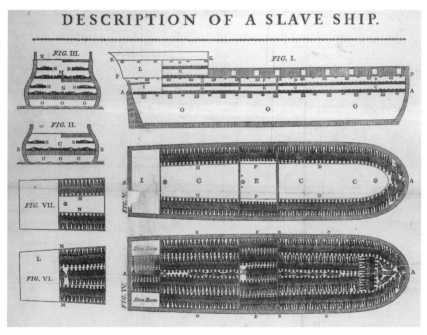

A diagram of the *Brooks* slave ship, which transported enslaved Africans to the Caribbean. The drawing showed the world how 609 Africans were tightly packed at sea in an area ten inches high, often chained or shackled together. The diagram appeared in newspapers in England in 1787 before being published around the world. It was instrumental in turning public opinion against the slave trade.

LEFT: Olaudah Equiano was an enslaved man who bought his freedom and wrote compellingly about his experiences. He was a prominent figure in the British abolitionist movement. *From Creative Commons.*

BELOW: Antietam National Cemetery. The Battle of Antietam (September 17, 1862) remains the bloodiest day in American history, with 22,717 dead, wounded, or missing. It was a turning point in the Civil War.

ABOVE: In 1791, Captain John Kimber of Bristol tortured to death an enslaved teenage girl who refused to dance naked on the deck of the *Recovery*. Kimber was tried for murder. Though he was found "innocent," this cartoon by Isaac Cruikshank led to growing opposition to the slave trade. BELOW: Concrete busts of enslaved Africans made by Ghanaian sculptor Kwame Akoto-Bamfo for his Ancestor Project. His art helps humanize the anonymous millions of trafficked Africans.

ABOVE: Diving With A Purpose ready to explore the Spanish slaver the *Guerrero* off the Florida Keys. The ship sank in 1827, illegally trafficking 561 enslaved people from West Africa to Cuba. BELOW: Divers Alannah Vellacott, Josh Williams, and Kinga Philipps examine human leg shackles from a slave ship discovered off the Florida Keys.

ABOVE: An iron anchor believed to be from the British antislavery patrol ship HMS *Nimble*, off the Florida Keys. It was lost in 1827, while chasing the illegal Spanish slaver the *Guerrero*. The slave trade had been abolished in England in 1808. BELOW: Marine archaeologist Corey Malcom finds a Spanish-style bar shot, a type of cannon projectile believed to be from the slave ship the *Guerrero*.

Samuel L. Jackson, Prof. Lee White, and archaeologist Dr. Richard Oslisly looking at millions of oyster shells spanning 2,500 acres in Loango National Park, Gabon. This food was a "last supper" for Africans prior to being forced to board European slave ships and trafficked across the Middle Passage to plantations in the Americas.

Alannah Vellacott and Kramer Wimberley's hunt for European slave ships ends by meeting the late civil rights leader and congressman John Lewis in Washington, DC.

I rise!

ENCHAINED

B ack on firm ground, air tanks were filled, buoyancy vests checked, dry suits fussed over for the tiniest of holes, and the ROV system taken apart and cleaned. The team was as prepared as it would ever be. The next day they steamed out of Mylor at the crack of dawn. Nobody likes heading to work at 4:00 A.M. The night-lights were still twinkling across town. Southwest Cornwall, home to the wizard Merlin, looked magical. Nobody had slept the night before. The team felt hungover. For the best chance of getting in and out before the punishing waves started rolling, this was the only window of opportunity.

The *Severn Sea* research ship had gone ahead to send the ROV over the side, relocate the wreck site and lay the groundwork. The team was on a speedboat in hot pursuit. The sea was seriously choppy. The tech divers tied down their equipment so it would not fly overboard. Others put their heads down to stop themselves being sick.

Richard Stevenson and Kieran Hatton rested as best they could and started visualizing the challenge ahead. They are two of the best rebreather divers in the world. Some say it's crazy, the dangers too great. Rebreather divers need to be as cool as a cucumber and obsessive-compulsive to make sure technology, mind, and environment are perfectly in tune. Deep divers go down with multiple backup systems—belts and braces. Like a parachute, everything has to be tested time and time again. There are dozens of diving fatalities every year. Many involve rebreathers.

Getting down would be the easy bit. By the time they would be ready to ascend, their bodies would be saturated with gas. To safely decompress, they would need to stop every three meters for one minute on the way up and then hang suspended at six meters below the surface for an hour. Ten minutes down. Three hours to get back. Crawling home from 110 meters and 340 years of time travel. All in a day's work.

Still the weather worsened. A heavy wave crashed over the deck. The speedboat was lifted high out of the sea and crashed down into the ocean valley before the next wave hit. The team hugged their raincoats tightly and pushed on toward the Western Approaches. Nobody was having any fun. This time warp reminded the team what the captain, crew, and enslaved Africans on 35F must have felt in their final minutes—pure terror.

If the weather was mean halfway out, conditions were atrocious over the wreck. The *Severn Sea* had made it and called in with bad news. The ship was being pounded by waves. The sea state was too heavy to launch the ROV. The team ran the risk of becoming the Narrow Seas' latest victim. Rich took the painful decision to can the dive. The perils were just too great.

The divers headed back to port empty-handed. The great storm Sean Kingsley had warned the team about had rolled into town with a vengeance. Waves the size of houses broke over Mylor's harbor sea wall. All Diving With A Purpose could do was batten down the hatches, wait out the storm, and daydream. The wreck was jealously guarding its historic secrets.

The weather reports promised this was just the beginning of a major storm front. The forecast was for at least four days of rain and havoc. The clock was ticking and the window of opportunity to dive Site 35F closing fast. The team could only pray for a lull between storms and then make a run for it. They had come too far not to prevail.

Raiding & Trading

The life and times of the sunken Royal African Company trader haunted the team's waking hours and dreams. How did a cargo of elephant tusks end up on this merchant ship? Were the copper manilla bracelets used to buy and enslave people in West Africa? The history behind the finds told a spine-chilling truth.

The Royal African Company acted like lords on the Gold Coast, even though England's powers had practical limits so far from home. To make sure Western society could start the day with two lumps of sugar in their tea and coffee, take hot cocoa in the afternoon, and so men could relax at night with a pipe filled with tobacco, meant fueling the plantations of the West Indies with a factory treadmill of manpower. The African trade flowed through a string of fourteen English forts, some ferocious, others mere "thatched hovels" with little defense. Finding and loading ivory could take 90 days, slaves 120 days. The forts were less about protection. Day-to-day they were giant holding pens.

Even in Africa, few captains had a clue where the human cargos they enslaved came from. Fort governors raised their eyebrows at the many languages the Africans spoke and that some were scarred with marks on their faces and bodies. They did not appreciate how they were cultural markers of different tribes and cultures. The capture of Africans took place far from the eyes of Europeans in the hands of West Africa's rulers.

The harsh reality was that everyone was to blame for the slave trade. Everyone had blood on their hands, including the English, Dutch, French, Portuguese, Spanish, Danes, Prussians, and even Africans. It was brought about by Europe's consumer greed. Without the West's obsessive needs, Africa's human population would have been left in peace.

Africans ended up trapped by many foul and deceptive ways. Ship captains dealt directly with African kings, rulers, and their brokers. If they were given advance notice, castle governors could guarantee slave cargos were already locked up and ready to sail as soon as favored customers made landfall, all for a handsome fee.

Most adventurers believed enslaved Africans were the spoils of wars between tribal kingdoms. In the years of feuding, as in 1681, an English captain could buy three hundred captives overnight "for nothing besides the trouble of receiving them at the beach in his boats" after enemies dragged captives "from the field of battle, having obtained a victory over a neighboring nation, and taken a great number of prisoners." When the inland country was at peace in 1682, the French failed to find a single captive to buy after three days of searching.

In his book *Description of Guinea* (1732), John Barbot, a French trading agent from Paris, similarly understood that

> Those sold by the Blacks are for the most part prisoners of
> war, taken either in fight, or pursuit, or in the incursions they
> make into their enemies territories; others stolen away by their
> own countrymen; and some there are, who will sell their own
> children, kindred, or neighbors.

Other native peoples were imprisoned by lies and treachery. After being hired to carry goods to the coast like leather hides and elephant teeth, many innocents ended up taken and sold at the tip of a spear. Men, women, and children might be stolen by neighboring kingdoms if they were caught alone on the open road or tending corn fields. At times of famine, some families had no option but to sell themselves or starve. Nothing in this chain was possible without the approval of the local rulers. Today, raiding and kidnapping, not wars, are thought to have been the main source of slave trafficking.

The kings of Accra in Ghana raked in fortunes from gold and slaves. In 1785 a Danish scientist visited an inland ruler who showed him a gold nugget so large it took four men to lift, so the story goes. Around 22 percent of all slaves exported to the Americas came from the Bight of Benin, where one million captives were sold in Whydah. In the 1680s, Barbados's plantation owners preferred workers from Ghana's Gold Coast, especially the River Gambia. Some estates paid £3 or £4 more per head for the Papa Africans of Whydah. The enslaved shipped from nearby Ardra in the Bight of Benin were also especially popular on sugar plantations, being, according to their owners, "lusty, strong, and very laborious people."

Deals were sealed a number of ways. In the Bight of Benin, captains were welcomed by 1,200 armed men dancing on the shore. Porters carried ships' officers to Ardra in hammocks for the price of four manillas a day. Negotiations began at Little Ardra when ship's agents called "supercargoes" gifted a king three or four pounds of fine coral, cloth, and silk. The Europeans then paid the kings the value of fifty slaves in imported goods in return for the right to trade. At Whydah, the price of captives was reckoned according to the number of a ship's masts. Three-mast ships paid rulers the equivalent of twenty-one slaves in European goods. Women cost a fourth or a fifth less than men. When the negotiations

were sealed, the town crier announced that every subject in the kingdom
was free to trade with the supercargo. European slave traders set off in
canoes along the shore in search of willing sellers.

In other towns, after a king reached terms, an iron bell was rung
and captives dragged in and sold on the spot. A surgeon would carefully examine the captives, force them to jump up and down and stretch
out their arms "to see that they were sound wind and limb." The doctor
would gape into the captives' mouths to check their teeth and age and
"our greatest care of all is to buy none that are pox'd [diseased], lest they
should infect the rest aboard."

In New Calabar in eastern Nigeria, Royal African Company merchants received kings on their ships. One ruler dressed in a worn-out
scarlet coat laced with gold and silver, a fine hat, and walking barefoot
was saluted with seven cannon shots when he came onboard an adven-
turer's ship in 1699. The ruler was presented with a new hat, a firelock
pistol, and nine bunches of beads. When negotiations were over, the
king's public crier blew a trumpet made from an elephant tusk to
announce permission to trade. Elsewhere, in Angola, deals might be
made in front of a prince seated on a great chair, shaven-headed and
naked under a black cloak and slippers. King and merchant shared palm
wine served in a silver cup.

Captives were bought using the local currency, copper and brass
manillas, or the thirty-six copper bars for a man and thirty for a
woman paid by the supercargo of the *Arthur* in 1678. The captain of
the *Hannibal* paid one hundred pounds weight of cowrie shells for one
slave in 1693.

In the eyes of the Africans, Europeans were all-powerful, with their
ships and guns. It was natural for African chiefs to barter with them for
prisoners. At first it never occurred to these chiefs that the people sold
into slavery would be regarded as chattel, property, less than human. By
the time kingdoms, like the Ashanti, realized what the Europeans were
up to, it was too late. They were complicit in an economic system that
traded European goods for African resources—gold, ivory, and people.

THE DOOR OF NO RETURN

After four days of waiting for the weather to break, the sea finally fell calm, a short relief before winter rolled into Cornwall with a vengeance. This was the last chance saloon. The orange-red sun rose over the Narrow Seas, lighting up the waters like a gift from above.

Once again, Diving With A Purpose and rebreather divers Rich Stevenson and Kieran Hatton raced toward Site 35F. The signs looked promising. The only bad omen was Kieran, who realized that he had forgotten to put on his lucky underpants that morning.

Alannah was excited. She could see the end of the tunnel. "I never would have imagined this opportunity to give a voice to the silenced, breathing new life into people of color who are still living with questions unanswered," she said, sharing the team's feelings.

The *Severn Sea* made it to the wreck site and called in a sea state report. Conditions were good. The dive was on. The ROV was safely lowered overboard and its lights turned on. Soon after, the dive team arrived and suited up.

Rich and Kieran's rebreather kit, four air tanks attached to their backs and sides, looked like something from a Hollywood sci-fi fantasy. They stepped into inner space and immediately plunged down a shot line dropped by the ROV, their only link between surface and seabed. Time was precious. There was no room for error. Getting lost could be fatal. A one-inch-thick piece of rope would be their only guide. The divers' lives hung on a wire.

Unlike open-circuit scuba, where every time you exhale you lose a lungful of gas, Rich and Kieran's rebreather tanks would re-loop the gas to turn it back into fresh air. Rebreathers let divers breathe the same lungful of gas over and over again. Their efficiency lets them dive deeper and longer. Even the Darth Vader noises of a scuba mouthpiece disappear. Rebreathers are so silent fish think divers just are bigger fish. They cannot hear you coming.

At 110 meters the water is like ink. An eternal night enveloped Rich and Kieran. Making out where you are, up or down, is impossible in this inner space. The divers had no benefit of sea-to-surface underwater communications speakers. They were isolated between the devil and the deep blue sea.

Getting to the wreck was a ten-minute commute with just a flashlight for company to show the way. The good news was there are no sharks in these seas. The bad news was the punishing cold. Deep diving is as much a state of mind as a physical activity. Finning ever deeper, like sportsmen visualizing a win, they got into the zone, thinking about the job at hand, what they needed to achieve and foreseeing any glitches. The rest of the team was geared up and on standby at the surface, ready to rush down extra oxygen tanks if trouble hit. Two thirds of diving fatalities happen in under three meters.

After seven minutes, faint beams of light from the divers' flashlights flickered on the ROV's video feed. Rich and Kieran had made it to a place no human had been before. A lone sea bass swam across the wreckage, unflustered by the alien invaders.

Within fifteen meters of the seabed the whole wreck opened up in a panoramic bird's-eye view. The ship's wooden sides had flattened out long ago like a filleted fish. A cluster of eight cannons welcomed Rich and Kieran, even though cut marks in their sides told a sad tale of fishing boat scallop dredge teeth still bulldozing the precious remains. The guns had been scrambled too, worryingly thrown around like matchsticks by fishing trawler gear since the last time robots visited Site 35F. Shredded parts of the wooden ship and strange concretions hiding invisible secrets lay all around.

Stubbornly refusing to give in to the inevitable, part of the fragile keelson—the ship's backbone—sat above the seabed as if it hoped one day to take off and sail again. There was little time to take in the glory. Rich and Kieran had just ten minutes to find the tusk, prepare it for lifting, and get out of there.

Tainted Blood

How did it come to this? Why did the Royal African Company and the West find it reasonable to treat human beings like cattle? In 1651, the Guinea Company instructed Englishman Bartholomew Howard to sail for West Africa and "buy and put aboard you so many negros as y'or ship can cary, and for what shal be wanting to supply with Cattel." Africans were reduced to the status of cargo and beasts of burden with no human rights.

Oxygen was first breathed into this hateful mindset in Spain. In Toledo, any hope that Africans converted to Catholicism might one day escape bondage, was shattered. In June 1449, a set of laws based on the "purity of a human's bloodline," the Sentencia-Estatuto, was signed by the magistrate of Toledo, Pedro Sarmiento, on behalf of the city cathedral. The legislation was meant to ferret out Jews and Muslims who had been forcibly converted to Christianity. After all, once they became Christians, technically speaking, there were no obstacles to their advancements.

So the new laws, for the first time in Europe, differentiated between people not on the basis of faith but blood. From now on what mattered was birth. Whether you were a Jew, a Muslim, or an African was one and the same. You were foreign, other, and stained. Only Christian Spaniards from a pure and uncontaminated bloodline, where all four grandparents were Spanish Christians, could work for the government, religious orders, or join guilds.

The new creed got the ultimate blessing. Pope Nicholas V signed a public letter in 1452 giving Spain's chief ally, Portugal, the right to enslave sub-Saharan Africans. The Church elders insisted slavery was a natural and righteous Christian way to stop the spread of barbarian behavior. And so King Afonso V of Portugal was given a green light to

> invade, search out, capture, vanquish, and subdue all Saracens [Muslims] and pagans whatsoever, and other enemies of Christ wheresoever placed, and the kingdoms, dukedoms, principalities, dominions, possessions, and all movable and immovable goods whatsoever held and possessed by them and to reduce their persons to perpetual slavery.

People with the wrong blood coursing through their veins could also be reduced to "perpetual slavery," even if they were Christians. The pope and king of Spain had unfurled the world's first racial profiling based on bloodline. Bad ideas can go a very long way. In the 1670s the Royal African Company latched onto Spain's thoughts on Africans as perpetual slaves. If it was good enough for the pope, it was good enough for King Charles II.

SLAVERY THROUGH THE AGES

Slavery has been a constant part of human history from Europe to the Middle East and China. It still persists today in places like Mauritania, Sudan, and India, where it is estimated that over fourteen million people, including women and children, are enslaved, working in quarries, farms, and brick kilns.

In biblical times, slavery was permitted but a master's power over a slave was restricted. As the Book of Leviticus puts it, "You may buy male and female slaves from among the nations that are around you. You may make slaves of them, but over your brothers, the people of Israel, you shall not rule, one over another ruthlessly." Nevertheless, activists like the prophet Nehemiah scolded wealthy Israelites for owning local slaves. The entire theme of the biblical narrative is antislavery.

The central story of the Hebrew Bible is the exodus and the emancipation of the Israelites from slavery in Egypt. Hebrew slaves had to be let go after six years and provided with the means of being free. Slaves—Hebrew and non-Hebrew—were also offered relief on the Sabbath. These innovations were without parallel in the ancient Near East. Non-Hebrew slaves were considered permanent acquisitions and never had to be freed. However, the Rabbinic Talmud argues that this does not give one the right to humiliate them: "Rabbi Samuel said: I gave them to you for work, but not for humiliation." The great Jewish philosopher Maimonides elaborated further how to "be compassionate and pursue justice, do not excessively burden slaves, nor cause them distress."

The Hebrew Bible is so powerfully antislavery—Moses is, in effect, an abolitionist leader—that slaves in the nineteenth-century American South were given Bibles that omitted most of the Old Testament. The so-called Slave Bible told the story of Joseph's enslavement, for example, but left out the parts where Moses stands up to authority, stating, "Thus says the Lord, the God of the Hebrews: Let my people go!" (Exodus 9:1). Because of this, many antislavery spirituals, such as "Go Down Moses," explicitly reference the Bible for inspiration.

Rome ran the largest slave society in the ancient world. Captives were enslaved from empire-wide wars as far as Britannia and the Balkans. In Roman Egypt around 15 percent of city residents were slaves and as many as two million across Italy. Slaves did not come cheap: an unskilled rural laborer might cost one thousand daily wages. The enslaved toiled in fields as estate managers, field hands, domestic staff, craftsmen, miners, clerks, teachers, doctors, midwives, potters, and entertainers.

Slaves could be kept in chains, turned into gladiators for entertainment, abused, and used for sexual services. Some did work their way up to positions of power, wealth, and freedom. Those who were granted *libertus* by their masters became citizens. They could vote and play a role in politics. Other freedmen became wealthy, such as the brothers who owned the fancy House of the Vettii in Pompeii, one of the city's most magnificent houses. It was a freedman who designed Pompeii's amphitheater. The ex-slave Trimalchio, who organized the finest dinner parties in the Roman world in Petronius's book *The Satyricon*, ended up inspiring the lead character in F. Scott Fitzgerald's *The Great Gatsby*.

Rome's fluid society was a far cry from the two centuries leading up to the American Civil War. Slavery may have been abolished in America, but Black people in the Southern states were still subject to segregation and oppression. Integration remained an impossible dream well into the twentieth century. Fundamentally, the difference

between antiquity and colonial Europe was that the special brand
of racial segregation seen in the transatlantic trade was not a
feature of earlier civilizations. The customs of earlier cultures
may have been abhorrent, but ancient empires did not industri-
ally mine an entire continent like Africa to enslave its people.

England added a dark religious spin to justify its actions. According to
the Church of England, Africa was condemned by God Almighty. Why?
Because Africans were descended from the Biblical Ham and his son
Canaan. In the Book of Genesis (9:25), Noah's son, Ham, made the dis-
respectful mistake of looking at his father's nakedness. For this sin, Noah
raged against Ham and his son Canaan: "Cursed be Canaan; a slave's slave
shall he be to his brethren." By declaring Africans "Hamites," the Church
of England was saying that Africans were destined for "eternal servitude."

The End of the Line

Over three thousand years after Noah's curse was recorded, his words
were used to justify one of the greatest atrocities in human history. Once
captured, Africans ended up enchained in the dungeons of castles like
Cape Coast and Elmina in Ghana, West Africa's most powerful forts.
The captives were locked in what the British described as spacious man-
sions, which were really dungeons "cut out of the rocky ground, arched
and divided into several rooms; so that it will conveniently contain a
thousand blacks, let down at an opening made for the purpose," explained
Jean Barbot, the French trade agent-general, in 1682.

In these dungeons, newly taken Africans were shackled in collars and
branded over their hearts with the initials DY, standing for their new
owner, the Duke of York and governor of the Royal African Company,
or the initials of the ship's name or captain. The captives and masters are
now long gone, the cries of anguish faded into thin air. The memories,
though, are still with us.

Very few African voices record the atrocities. Quobna Ottobah
Cugoano, born in the Fante village of Ajumako in 1757 and kidnapped

at the age of thirteen, is one of the exceptions. Cugoano was traded to England, rechristened John Stuart, and ended up writing a diary about his scarring experiences, *Thoughts and Sentiments on the Evil and Wicked Trade of the Slavery and Commerce of the Human Species* (1787). The youngster had been sold into bondage in Cape Coast Castle, where he was petrified the English planned to eat him. He was locked up in the dungeon for three days where he "heard the groans and cries of many . . . when a vessel arrived to conduct us away to the ship, it was a most horrible scene; there was nothing to be heard but rattling of chains, smacking of whips, and groans and cries of our fellow men . . ."

On their forced march to the shore, many Africans dug their nails into their home soil. Crews kept them shackled between the forts and ship holds and while they were in sight of the coast of Africa. This was where captives tried their hardest to escape or mutiny. At times, captains cut the legs and arms off the most rebellious Africans "to terrify the rest, for they believe if they lose a member, they cannot return home again."

Twelve captives trafficked to the English ship the *Hannibal* in 1694 refused to go quietly and accept a future worse than death, so its captain wrote:

> The negroes are so wilful and loth to leave their own country, that they have often leap'd out of the canoes, boat and ship, into the sea, and kept under water till they were drowned . . . they having a more dreadful apprehension of Barbadoes than we can have of hell . . .

The English and other Europeans may have lived behind silk curtains, and dined off silver plates, but civilization had long deserted these shores. In both Cape Coast and Elmina Castles, the governors' bedrooms led by a secret passageway to the women's dungeons. Female slaves would be picked out for the governor's personal "inspection" and raped. Life was cheap and governors made merry while they could. Nobody stopped them. Nobody wrote about the violations. They were kept out of governors' and captains' logs. What happened in Africa stayed in Africa. Besides, if the women became pregnant, all the better. There would be another child to sell at journey's end.

Elmina Castle, with its gleaming whitewashed stone walls, was the last sight the enslaved saw of their homeland. Ahead waited the fearful Middle Passage between West Africa and the West Indies, the plantations, and eternal slavery. Crossing these seas, 1.8 million enslaved Africans would die.

At Elmina, captives were held in an airless hole in the ground. To enter you had to pass the castle's church, acknowledging the all-seeing Christian God and bend over in surrender to almost crawl through an arched passageway. This dark, dirty space was the end of the line, the end of freedom.

A small sliver of light shone through the chilling Door of No Return, guarded by an iron gate, at its center a cross, the sign of Christ's compassion. Thirty thousand slaves a year were prodded, one by one, through this one-way door. Once the enslaved passed this point, it marked the end of their culture. Their names would be changed. They faced a life of forced labor and their children and children's children would be born into slavery. More than half the Africans trafficked in the transatlantic trade passed through Elmina's sea gate.

THE ELMINA SHIPWRECK

The approaches to Elmina Castle in Ghana saw many disasters. In the 1580s, Portuguese galleys attacked a French fleet, sinking the *Esperance*. The British brig *James Matthews* was lost off Elmina in 1766. The crew and six slaves escaped to shore, only to be stripped naked by the locals. A reef running eight hundred meters offshore was a natural ship trap to be approached with great caution.

A mile and a half off Elmina, an armed Dutch ship was lost in sight of the castle stocked with remains of a rich cargo ready to trade: 34 stacks of brass basins, brass pins, over 3,800 glass beads, 636 manillas, pewter basins, and cowrie shells have been found. The ship is thought to be the Dutch West India Company's *Groningen*, lost in 1647 after catching fire when a cannon exploded during a salute to Elmina Castle.

A letter written by Hendrick Caarlof, the governor of Elmina, on March 5, 1647, describes how "the ship Groeningen . . . wished to fire 5 shots, as is customary, had caught fire from the last cannon, which had burst . . . The hatch of the orlop flew overboard; but the worst of all was that the blow took its chief force downwards . . . The descending fire progressing so strongly caused the crew, through sheer amazement to get into perplexity . . . 11 seamen and eight soldiers perished in the fire. In the blowing up of the ship some goods flew up and got into the hands of the Blacks, part of which has been taken from them, and some fished up by dredging, which we will continue to do . . ."

When the Dutch West India Company was founded in 1621, its directors at first refused to trade in humans as immoral. The Dutch changed their mind by the mid-1630s and committed to the slave trade. From 1674 to 1730, the company signed 383 slave trade ventures.

Today, the hatred has flown from the white walls of Elmina. The English have gone home, along with the rest of colonial Europe. Since then, Britain has apologized for the slave trade. The Netherlands, Germany, and America have apologized. So has the pope, the Church of England, the Bank of England, and the world's biggest insurance company, Lloyd's of London. West Africa, Benin, Ghana, Nigeria, and Uganda have also apologized for their role in the slave trade. South Africa has apologized. But are apologies enough? They slam the lid shut on the dark past, rather than seeking creative ways to make sure the world never forgets.

The Royal Bubble Bursts

The Royal African Company's cozy deal did not last long. The organization that sent the 35F ship to West Africa was a blazing financial comet. It burned brightly before fizzing out. The company turned out to be a monster with sprawling overheads and ambitions that it could not sustain.

The company had to fight to keep its royal rights. Few liked the powers wielded by the pro-French Catholic Duke of York, the governor of the Royal African Company and heir to the crown. England was a land for Protestants. The company behaved like a divinely sanctioned bully, far too big for its boots. Branding any English ship trading independently a pirate spread unease across the British Isles.

Little wonder skippers skimmed profits by smuggling extra slaves and cargos. The company's finances were a nightmare to juggle. The king's men were required to maintain the string of Gold Coast forts for Britain's foreign interests. But they were not given anywhere near enough government funds for the upkeep of bricks, mortar, guns, and officials.

Cash flow was a problem. The company sold slaves to its Caribbean colonies on credit. The floating debt was never easy to recover from far-off planters. The Royal African Company was a bureaucratic nightmare as well. Independent traders could complete two journeys to Guinea and back in the time it took London to get a single ship readied.

War with France made safe passage tricky, as enemy corsairs from Saint-Malo preyed on English merchant shipping. The Royal African Company managed to lose 114 ships from 1689 to 1708 to storms, wrecks, and the enemy, raking up losses of £124,652 or $18.3 million today.

The biggest nail in the company's coffin was the feeling of unfair play. To the great coastal cities—Liverpool, Bristol, and Lancaster—the royal monopoly violated the natural human right to free trade, the very bastion on which Britain was built. Corporations like Bristol's Society of Merchant Venturers sent petitions to London demanding change.

After just twenty-six years of trading, the Royal African Company was beaten. The Act to Settle the Trade to Africa signed in 1698 opened up Africa to all adventurers for a small fee: "Any Subjects as well as the Company may trade to Africa between Cape Blanco and Cape Mount, paying £10 per Cent. for Goods exported; And £10 per Cent. on all Goods, &c. imported into England or America, from Africa." Now everyone could get into the African trafficking business.

Facing the Atlantic on England's southwestern shore, Bristol was perfectly placed to knock London off its arrogant slave-trading perch. After 1698 the city played a major role in the transatlantic slave trade. Its merchants backed over two thousand voyages trafficking more than half a million enslaved Africans to the Americas. By the 1730s, thirty-six slave voyages left Bristol a year, rising to fifty-three at the end of the decade. Bristol had got its hands on 40 percent of Britain's slave trade. With its forest of ships' masts bobbing in the channel down to the sea, Bristol was built on the back of enslaved Africans. The whole city gladly took an economic shot in the arm—shipbuilders, merchants, tradesmen, manufacturers, bankers, and small-time investors. Prosperity snowballed. The city made and sold guns, brass goods, booze, cloth, hats, and fancy goods for the Guinea trade. The Warmley Brass Company exported cooking pots. The Bristol Brass and Copper Company cast manilla bracelets.

Newly docked sugar had to be refined, tobacco and indigo processed, and chocolate manufactured from cargos of cacao. Thousands worked for the slave trade machine, which gave birth to Bristol's first banks, whose profits landscaped the city with the finest architecture from warehouses to churches. Bristol, the metropolis of the West, enjoyed a golden age.

Despite the depth of slavery's influence, the finger of blame is pointed today at one man—Edward Colston. His name is everywhere in the city—Colston's Almshouses, Colston Tower, Colston Street, Colston's Girls' School. The Colston bun, a sweet bun made of yeast dough flavoured with fruits and spices, still honors his legacy. How did Britain's most hated historic figure of recent memory, who got rich from human suffering, become so famous and then infamous?

Colston's cash was bloodstained from his inside trading as a fixer, enforcer, and in 1689 deputy governor of the Royal African Company. In the years he worked for the company, 84,500 enslaved African men, women, and children were branded and sold in the Caribbean and Americas. Up to 19,300 died crossing the Middle Passage.

Back in the day, everyone loved Edward Colston, who was one of the country's great philanthropists. In his lifetime he donated £63,940 to charities, including hospitals, almshouses and churches. He left another £71,000 to grand causes when he breathed his last in 1721 ($22.1 million in modern money). Everyone revered and respected the humble Colston, a man who refused to marry and left instructions to be buried in a simple grave. When people sniggered behind his back at his lack of a bride, he quipped that "every helpless widow is my wife and her distressed orphans my children." He doled out cash to old helpless sailors. When he died, aged eighty-four, the bells of Bristol rang for sixteen hours straight. Colston's obituary called him "the highest example of Christian liberality that this age has produced, both for the extensiveness of his charities and the prudent regulation of them."

In the twenty-first century, Colston's reputation lies in tatters. As we now know, his "Christian liberality" was made possible by his involvement in the slave trade. The grand statue the city set up in his honor was ripped down and slung in Bristol harbor at the height of England's Black Lives Matter protests in 2020. A new conversation is now underway about Britain's guilt in the transatlantic slave trade and how it should remember and mark past evils.

Bristol's conflicted history is perfectly summed up today by the poet and educator Lawrence Hoo's *Inner City Tales*:

> *Now Edward Colston is held as the beacon for this trade. When the reality is that through it, Bristol was made.*
>
> *Bristol profited so many ways, to name them all would take us days.*
>
> *But trade, commerce, and stature is to name just a few. On the power of the African people's suffering, Bristol grew.*
>
> *Imagine not being allowed to speak in your natural tongue. Imagine not being allowed to educate your young.*
>
> *Then, over time, your ways are lost and your history is forgotten, and you become a part of a world where you belong at the bottom.*
>
> *The people who did it said they're the civilized race. They keep rewriting history to make their case.*
>
> *But if we look at the facts and the facts alone. Who was uncivilized and savage is easily shown.*

By 1701 the Royal African Company's share in the slave trade had plummeted to 8 percent from a high of 88 percent in 1690. Bristol had disrupted and overtaken London's position as Britain's top slave trading city. Profititing from trafficking innocent Africans was no longer an elite pursuit. Rather, it was now in every Englishman's economic interest.

White Gold

Kramer waited, suspended in the shallows of the English Channel. Had Rich and Kieran found one of the wrecked elephant tusks and would it see the light of day, safe and sound? *Those two gentlemen are in a place where no one else has ever been*, he thought. Josh was struggling to make sense of past and present. He knew he was literally free diving above a sunken graveyard that may have entombed his ancestors, who were anything but free.

Time passed painfully slowly. The divers had spent just twenty minutes on the sea bottom. The tiptoe ascent would take another two and a half hours of decompression. You can fly from New York to Miami in the time Rich and Kieran would need to claw their way back from the sunken past.

Finally, telltale jellyfish-shaped air bubbles rose from the oblivion below. Diving With A Purpose had set up a final decompression station six meters below the surface. Emergency gas tanks filled with 100 percent oxygen were tied to the sides of a bar Rich and Kieran could hang onto and start to relax. They were too exhausted battling strong currents to celebrate. All they could do was wait for the inert gas their bodies had absorbed to be released. Another hour of decompression to go.

When their bloodstreams returned to normal, the divers clambered gratefully onto their speedboat. Rich peeled the hood off his dry suit and blinked, pasty looking, in the midday sun. It would take time for the ancient dust to settle. It was too soon to make sense of where they had been, what they had achieved. Rich sighed, humbled by the history-making dive, and told his friends that "to be enlightened is my motivation to spend four hours in the freezing water. That's my personal reward."

The living were safe. It was time to check in with the ancestors. On the seabed, the elephant tusk had been liberated from its sandy tomb by light hand fanning and secured in a custom-built padded lifting basket. The team took turns hauling up by hand the tusk attached to the rope line. Their muscles ached in sympathy with the pain the Africans trafficked on this Royal African Company ship felt toiling in Caribbean plantations.

The 340-year-old tusk pillaged from Africa, along with millions of Africans, was hauled over the side of the *Severn Sea*. The team stared in wonder, shock, and anger. Seaweed and sand covered the artifact, but it was clearly a curved elephant's tusk. The hard dentin of its tooth had preserved it for all time, a fossil of England's role in the slave trade.

Europe's lust for what it called luxurious white gold took a heavy environmental toll. The greed for luxury and profit was a pandemic that spread from the savannah grasslands of Ghana to the streets of London, Paris, and Amsterdam. As time went by, the majestic sight of elephants faded from the map. Today, the long shadow of the ivory trade has reached the end of the line, too. Three and a half million elephants once roamed wild. Seventy percent are now gone. Africa's elephants are on the edge of extinction and it all started with English and Dutch ships like 35F in the seventeenth century.

WHITE GOLD

Three million elephants ended up slaughtered and their tusks stowed in European slave ships. White gold was a high-end luxury used to make statues, medallions, and fancy furniture. Ivory's soft, satiny surface was perfect for cutting tiny details for portraits and busts paid for by high society's deep pockets.

Ivory carving was a popular fashion in London, Germany, and Dieppe in France. Queen Anne, King George I, Sir Isaac Newton, Christopher Wren, and Samuel Pepys sat for ivory busts made by David Le Marchand, a Frenchman who fled religious persecution to London. In 1639 the German master craftsman Marcus Heiden created the wonder of the age for his Saxon duke masters: a drinking vessel perched on an elephant and topped with a ship under full sail. Tusks could be turned into a dizzying selection of exotic goods, from combs and knife handles to keys for clavichords and medical syringes. If you could afford it, from the 1700s you could buy lifelike ivory eyeballs, prosthetic limbs, false teeth to spare your mouth's rotten immodesty, artificial legs, noses, and, for the challenged male, even ivory penises.

Raw emotions hidden deep in the divers' souls bubbled to the surface. Private emotions for Kramer, Alannah, Josh, and Kinga. But most of all, emotions for the ancestors. Voice could finally be given to the enslaved.

For Alannah, the tusk symbolized the full circle of hundreds of years of suffering. She could now touch and sense the enslaved trafficked on hundreds of ships like this. Every captive had a mother, a father, a name, all ripped away from them. "They were people," Alannah choked emotionally. "I can't imagine being taken away from my family. I cannot fathom being taken across oceans I didn't even know existed. And then to be beaten and thrown about and be yelled at in a language I don't even understand and be told to do things I do not want to do."

For Kramer, this was just the start of righting injustice. "If it's the final resting place of some of my ancestors, then it's a burial ground," he told the team. "But it's also a crime scene because they were taken. There was an injustice that took place, and no one has ever been brought to account for that. I want justice for those people."

"It always bothers me to use the language 'slaves' on the ships," Kramer went on. "People speak in terms of the Africans in the ships as if they started out as slaves. They weren't slaves, they were Africans who were *enslaved*. There are generations who think that African history started with slavery. African history didn't start with African slavery. African history was interrupted by African slavery."

The profound shift from chasing gold and tusks to hunting slaves in the mid–seventeenth century struck a fatal blow for West Africa's destiny. Its economy and industry were held back for two hundred years. While the West raked in cash, Africa was locked in one of history's darkest ages. Feeding Europe's sweet tooth and smoking pipes opened the door to centuries of warlords that divided Africa, and still does in some regions.

The team took turns holding the resurrected tusk. It had traveled out of Africa on an English ship that sold most of its captives on the plantation islands of Barbados, Jamaica, and Nevis. Then it headed to London, possibly accompanied by a few slaves held back for the local market, the unsold outbound manillas, additional elephant tusks and almost certainly sugar and maybe gold. As the divers held the tusk, they felt a victory of sorts; free people holding ivory that was once worth more than the lives of their ancestors.

NEW WORLD CULTURES

We lookee and lookee and lookee and lookee

and we doan see nothin' but water.

Where we come from we doan know.

Where we goin, we doan know.

De boat we on called de Clotilde . . .

De water . . . It growl lak de thousand beastes

in de bush . . .

Sometime de ship way up in de sky.

Sometimes it way down in de bottom of de sea . . .

—Kazoola remembers in Zora Neale Hurston,

Barracoon: The Story of the Last "Black Cargo" (2018)

SANCTUARY

D own a twisting road, Alannah, Kramer, and Kinga wound their way along the coast of Costa Rica in blue and white Land Rovers. To the left rolled the Caribbean Sea; to the right rose mountains and dense tropical rainforest. The landscape was the wildest that Diving With A Purpose had confronted so far. The Land Rovers plunged and rocked through fjords swollen by winter rain and jangled over rickety wooden bridges. Monkeys and alligators glared at them. Locals on motorbikes swerved dangerously across the road. Women sliced jackfruit off trees with sharp machetes.

The divers' destination was Aditibri Suretka, several hours inland in southern Costa Rica. Today this land lies in the territory of the Bribri, an Indigenous people who have lived here for centuries. The Bribri are one of the most isolated of Costa Rica's eight Indigenous groups. Their thirty-five thousand people grow their own crops and have kept their language and culture alive.

The team had come to Costa Rica to meet a local group of young Bribri divers who believe Africans are a central part of their past. This time Diving With A Purpose were not investigating the deaths of those who never made it. They were investigating a group that may have beaten the odds and survived.

Most people will tell you the Bribri are descended from Mayans. But there is a another twist to the tale. As the Land Rovers cautiously headed uphill to Aditibri Suretka, Alannah told the team how "Their folklore tells of slave ships that were wrecked on the Costa Rican shoreline and of Africans who came ashore to make a new life for themselves in the forests. But their African ancestry has always been considered to be a mere tribal legend."

The human rights activist Maria Suárez Toro had invited the dive team to a Bribri feast to try and help the Bribri community reclaim the truth about their past by helping local teens dive slave ships off the coast. The Land Rovers parked among simple houses with corrugated roofs scattered among banana trees. After the introductions were over, and the feast underway, Maria took to her feet to talk about the legend of Africans arriving among the Bribri much earlier than previously thought. Just looking at one another's faces, these Bribri have often wondered about their color and wavy hair, glancing east across the Middle Passage to Africa.

Don Alejandro Swaby, a Bribri elder, may have been clad in his Indigenous group's traditional embroidered shirt but he told the visitors, "I have Black ancestry and I am proud of that. And that is the history we pass on to our kids. And it's the history that should be written for the future."

Kramer thanked the villagers for sharing their story and added that "On some level, I'm jealous because my question is always 'where do you come from?' And the answer to that for me is always 'I don't know.' I don't have a connection to my home or my people. So, to be able to assist in answering those questions is a connection for me."

Standing quietly on the side lines, Laura Wilson, an expert in local folklore, watched with great satisfaction as the descendants of Africans living far apart rubbed shoulders. Alannah asked Laura to share the locals' story about what happened on the slavers supposedly wrecked off Costa Rica.

Laura explained that "What we have heard of those ships that are at the bottom of the sea: Africans came to our area. These Africans came on a boat that gets wrecked on a beach where they know no one. You know, it's disastrous. You don't know where you're going. You don't know where you went to sleep."

Alannah found it hard to visualize being uprooted in this way. "I can't really imagine. You've just wrecked up in the middle of nowhere. You have no idea where you are. You look to your left and it's just ocean.

And then you look to your right and you see dark forest and you have to make a choice. Do you try and go back to the wreck or do you go into the rainforest? That must have been absolutely terrifying."

Laura shuddered. "This story is bringing me back to horrible things," she admitted. "You know, slavery was very horrible. Taking you out of your own homeplace and you don't know where you're going. There was nowhere else but to go but to adapt themselves with the Bribri and the other Indigenous folks that we had around here. As a kid in school, they didn't teach us that."

"They went into the rainforest and the Bribri adopted them. That's an amazing story," Alannah replied, before moving the story along. "From time to time, teenage divers have seen artifacts offshore. If we can connect them to slave ships, we will be able to back up the legends with hard evidence."

To the escaped captives, the tropical climate of the Mosquito Coast's lagoons, savannas, and rainforests must have felt very much like parts of West Africa. Into the modern day, many words used along the Mosquito Coast still have African roots. The enslaved carried their language into exile where they entered modern speech. Sweet potato yams spread West with the Fulani people. Gumbo, a culinary calling card of Louisiana, is borrowed from the Bantu *gumbos*. The cockroach takes its name from the West African *cacarootch*. Honeybees are believed to come from the Yoruba *honi*. *Todi* and *babuun* gave the West the frog and monkey. Jonathan Swift claimed to have invented the word *yahoo* in *Gulliver's Travels* in 1726 for a race of brutes, although it sounds surprisingly close to—and twisted from—a West African devil, *yahue*.

Legends of Danish Slavers

Most people in Costa Rica do not take the folklore about the Bribri's Black ancestry seriously. Sounds too much like a tall tale. But marine archeologist Andreas Bloch thinks differently. He may even have identified the precise ships the legends talk about. Clues back home in the archives in Denmark set him and his fellow researchers on a remarkable journey.

CHRISTIANUS QUINTUS & FREDERICUS QUARTUS

- *Christianus Quintus*, 35.9 meters long, 7.9 meters wide
- Named in honor of the Danish king, 1670–1699
- Built in Larvik, Norway
- Commanded by Captain Hans Hansen Maas, Jost van de Vogel, and later Anders Pedersen Waerøe
- Traded for gold, slaves, and ivory on the Gold Coast in 1699, 1703, and 1709
- *Fredericus Quartus*, 43.8 meters long
- Named in honor of King Frederik IV, 1699–1730
- Built in Copenhagen
- Commanded by Captain Dirk Fijfe
- Both ships carried twenty-four cannons and were manned by sixty men
- On their final voyage, the frigates left Denmark in December 1708 with cargos of sheets, guns, knives, Norwegian and Swedish iron, and cases of gifts, including cowrie shells and copper manilla bracelets
- Burnt and scuttled at Cahuita, Costa Rica, March 1710

Maria Suárez Toro, Kramer, Kinga, and Alannah met Andreas down by the shore near the Punta Cahuita. In this idyllic setting, the waves softly crashed onto the shore. Roosters crowed in the undergrowth. Andreas was poring over ancient cargo lists and comparing old maps of the region with aerial photos of the landscape today.

From her wreck dives so far, Alannah knew all about the history of England, America, Spain, and Holland in the slave trade. But she told Andreas she had no idea Denmark was also involved in trafficking Africans.

Andreas has researched lots of finds, from the Vikings of Denmark onward. He admitted, though, that even experts know little about Denmark and the slave trade. "Actually, I didn't know how large scale we were involved in the slave trade. I couldn't believe when I started looking at what had been written. Scholars believe that two specific slave ships made it to this coast. I think they're right."

"Looking at the material, they left Copenhagen in 1708. *Christianus Quintus* and *Fredericus Quartus*," he continued. "They're going to go to West Africa, to get slaves, and then transport them to the West Indies. When they leave West Africa, they are in bad weather conditions. They're completely lost in open waters for days and days. And they end up about here," Andreas ended, pointing toward the shore.

The *Christianus Quintus*, commanded by Captains Hans Hansen Maas, Jost van de Vogel, and later Anders Pedersen Waerøe, and Captain Dirk Fijfe on the *Fredericus Quartus*, sailed from Copenhagen in December 1708, each with a crew of sixty men. The frigates were owned by the Danish West India Guinea Company, part of its fleet of twenty slavers. Denmark usually sent two ships together—safety in numbers—to cover risks of mutiny, storms, and piracy. In the three decades from 1698, around 9,300 slaves were trafficked on Danish ships to the West Indies.

The frigates were contracted to deliver Africans to the company's vice commander, Jochum von Holten, on the small Danish island colony of Saint Thomas in today's US Virgin Islands. On their arrival at Cape Three Points in West Africa in March 1709, the captains' run of bad luck began. Relations had soured between the Akwamu empire in Ghana and Denmark's governor in Fort Christiansborg at Accra. The *Christianus Quintus* and *Fredericus Quartus* could not find enough captives locally. So, they were forced to hunt people and ivory as far east as Whydah in the Bight of Benin, two hundred miles away.

DANISH FORT CHRISTIANSBORG, GOLD COAST

Sweden built Christiansborg in 1652 to lodge staff and store goods. Denmark bought the land under the lodge from the local Ga Paramount chief, Okaikoi, for 3,200 gold florins ten years later. They upgraded it into a stone fort and called it Fort Christiansborg after

King Christian IV. Enlargements transformed the building into a castle with storage and living space, as well as impregnable defenses.

Christiansborg contained a courtyard, cistern, chapel, "mulatto school," storerooms and living quarters, a bell tower, and twenty-eight defensive cannon. In the castle lived the governor, bookkeeper, physician, and chaplain, protected by a garrison of Danes and Africans. Christiansborg Castle became Denmark's headquarters on the Gold Coast. The Danish transatlantic slave trade ended in March 1792 but was only enforced in 1803. The Danes claimed to be the world's first nation to abolish the trade. Denmark sold Christiansborg to the British for £10,000 in 1850.

Onboard the *Christianus* was an outbound cargo of 2,400 copper manilla bracelets, cloth, metal wares, and weapons to barter for goods. In the lower hold building materials were destined to repair and enlarge the Danish fort on Saint Thomas. The *Fredericus* was stocked with thirty chests of sheets, eight chests of "Dane-guns" especially loved by local rulers, two casks of knives, 1,170 bars of Norwegian and Swedish iron, and nineteen cases of curiosities. Four chests of blue paper would be used to pack West Indies sugar for the home crossing. For the long triangular voyage, the ship's stores included twenty-five thousand pounds of hard bread, three thousand pounds of soft bread, and twenty-two pounds of salted pork.

DANISH ST. THOMAS ISLAND, WEST INDIES

The Virgin Islands were "discovered" in Christopher Columbus's second voyage in 1493. Denmark colonized St. Thomas Island—half a mile long and two and a half miles wide—in 1672, the intended destination of the *Christianus Quintus* and *Fredericus Quartus* frigates' African captives. In 1673 the Danish West Indies Company sent a ship to Guinea to take 103 captives to work the island's cotton, sugar, and indigo plantations and kill-devil rum factories. By 1691 the island had a population of 212 men and women, 177 children, and 555 African slaves. Eighty-seven ships landed captives between 1687 and 1754. In 1705 the *Cron Printzen* left Fort Christiansborg in Ghana for St. Thomas with 820 Africans, the largest Danish shipment from Guinea to St. Thomas. Smallpox killed many, then a fire broke out in the gunpowder room in the Gulf of Guinea and the ship exploded. Only five men were saved. Two overcrowded Danish slavers reached St. Thomas in 1793, only to be destroyed by a hurricane at the harbor entrance. Nobody survived. The *Frederick III*'s 630 enslaved trafficked in 1696 was the island's largest successful "shipment."

Pirates were a more constant danger than shipwrecks. In the years when the *Christianus* and *Fredericus* sailed, St. Thomas was one of the Americas' most feared pirate lairs, where the likes of Henry Morgan, Henry Avery, William Kidd, Jean Hamlin, and George Bond raided and traded. The colony's early Danish governors cut deals with the pirates to let them use the port and warehouses. Denmark was politically neutral at the time. St. Thomas became a major slave market for all nations across the West Indies.

St. Thomas's harbor in Long Bay was one of the finest of the American islands, at times sheltering two hundred ships. The five-story-high Fort Christian was built in 1689 to house a hundred men. Its four bastions were armed with four cannons. Flag Tower and North Tower looked far out to see for trouble and trade. The governor lived inside the fort "like a viceroy," along with his government and privy council. The island was home to three towns, Charlotte Amalie, the Brandenburgery, and the so-called Negro Village.

At Little Popo in modern Togo, the curse struck again. The *Christianus* was loading captives and elephant tusks when a canoe capsized in the surf, killing the captain, a priest, and a trader. The first mate died soon after from a tropical illness. The inexperienced Anders Pedersen Waerøe, aged in his twenties, was left in command.

The *Fredericus* was also in trouble. The frigate had been delayed so long that the ship's stores were running dry. While boarding captives

from Fort Prinsensten in Keta in Ghana, the malnourished and rest-
less Africans broke free of their shackles and attacked their captors on
the night of September 13, 1709. The rebellion did not last long. The
hands of the mutiny's leader were cut off. Then he was decapitated,
his body hanged from the rigging to scare the rest of the Africans
into obedience.

PUNISHMENT FOR RUNAWAY SLAVES, DANISH ST. THOMAS

A Danish Royal Council decree, dated January 31, 1733, to stop
slaves escaping from St. Thomas (now the US Virgin Islands):
"The leader of runaway slaves shall be pinched three times with
red-hot iron and then hung. Each other runaway slave shall
lose one leg, or if the owner pardon him, shall lose one ear, and
receive one hundred and fifty stripes . . . A slave who runs away
for eight days, shall have 150 stripes, twelve weeks shall lose a
leg, and six months shall forfeit life, unless the owner pardon him
with the loss of one leg . . . A slave meeting a white person, shall
step aside, and wait until he passes; if not, he may be flogged . . .
Witchcraft shall be punished with flogging . . . All dances, feasts,
and plays are forbidden unless permission be obtained from the
master or overseer."

After months of searching the coast, the *Christianus* took onboard
373 captives (49 percent men, 46 percent women) and the *Fredericus*
embarked 433 Africans (52 percent men, 36 percent women). They
paid 52–54 silver rix-dollars for a male and 36–40 rix-dollars per woman.
The ship was divided into four rooms, twenty-five feet for cargo, and three
others separating the men, women, girls and boys, measuring forty-five
feet, ten feet, and twenty-two feet, respectively. In these tight spaces,
the captives' skin fell off at the elbows, hips, and shoulders rubbing
on the deck plank as the ship swayed from side to side.

A temporary wooden space to house the Africans on deck was lashed
together from mast to mast. Rigging spars were covered with light

matting to let a breeze blow through the makeshift jail, protecting the Africans from sun and rain and stopping them jumping overboard. Near the main mast the crew built a *barricado* from wooden boards, eight feet high, running from port to starboard. Cannon-sized portholes were cut into the barricade, ready for the crew to fire blunderbusses and prevent mutinies if they needed to retreat and protect themselves.

On the deck the captives were exercised, whipped, and forced to dance to music and drumming. The women were given beads to string as a diversion. The crews were under strict orders from the Danish Company directors to treat their captives like small children with regular food, fresh air, and singing and dancing. The Africans were washed and groomed daily to remove vermin, their quarters fumigated with Scandinavian juniper berries. Sexual abuse was supposedly forbidden.

Because they failed to round up the commissioned size of cargo, the ships topped up their hold with one hundred marks of gold and eight thousand pounds of elephant tusks. The troubles hounded them after leaving West Africa in October 1709, when the captains hoped to take on supplies on the Portuguese island of São Tomé. Bad weather made landing dangerous. The ships were forced to head to French-held Cape Lopez in Gabon. When word reached them that France and Denmark were at war, they lifted anchor at once and left without stopping for the West Indies with dwindling rations and many captives ill from malnutrition.

End of the Line

The Bribri teenagers, members of a local dive club, joined the team's discussions, eager to hear what Andreas thought about the legend of their African ancestry. The name of this spot, past and present, was a major clue.

"One of the reasons that we note the two ships could be here," Andreas explained, "is because in the Danish archives the name Carato is mentioned. That was where they ended up, close to the port of Carato. But that doesn't exist. So Carato sounds a lot like our Cahuita, and that is one of the reasons that it could be here. From the historical records, we know that the crews of the *Fredericus* and the *Christianus* anchored the ships close to shore and then mutinied against their captains."

"The conditions on board were horrendous," Andreas went on. "There was no food, no water. And they were afraid to die. The *Fredericus* was set on fire and the crew on the *Christianus* cut the anchor and the ship ran aground. The objects on board sank with the ships and scattered across the ocean floor. Most of the Africans were set ashore. So, these might be some of the first Africans coming to this area and populating it."

Eighteenth-century maps called the area where the jumbled wreckage lies off Cahuita "Pt. Carrett" and "Point Carata." Andreas, Diving With A Purpose, and especially the Bribri youth were hoping that a name sounding like "Cahuita" was not just a coincidence.

In local folklore, the African captives took to the forests. Many were never seen again. Fast-forward half a century to 1757 and Captain Robert Hodgson, the English superintendent on the Mosquito Coast, wrote a different version of the story:

> The natives, or Mosquito people, are of two breeds; one are the original Indian; the other (who are called the Samboes), a mixture of these with negroes, occasioned, so far as can be learned, by two Dutch ships full of them being cast away some years ago to the southward of Nicaragua, from whence the negroes travelled to the Mosquito country, where, after several battles, they had wives and ground given them; since which their posterity are become as numerous as the others, and there is now no distinction either in their rights or customs.

In the Bribri clan system, if a woman had a Black child, it was accepted by everyone and was considered Indigenous, neither Black nor African. The father's ethnicity or skin color made no difference. The Bribri divers were hoping the wreckage off Cahuita and Captain Hodgson's account beat a path to their existence in the here and now.

Salvador van Dyke, one of the Bribri teenagers, had noticed lots of artifacts of all ages off the local coast. He wanted to know, "How can we link all these objects to that time period in which these ships actually shipwrecked here?"

Andreas explained the plan to dive and find clues linking the artifacts by date or origin to the two lost Danish slave wrecks.

Kinga was intrigued by the spidery writing covering a particular historical document open in front of where Andreas was sitting at a table by the shore. "This looks like a cargo list. Is that correct?" she asked, pushing her sunglasses onto the top of her head. Everything stocked on the *Christianus Quintus* and *Fredericus Quartus* was meticulously logged before the ships left port.

"It is," Andreas confirmed. "We can see there's loads of different stuff here. There's pieces of canvas, and there's clothes, handguns, timbers, and bottles of wine and brandy."

"What key pieces of information and evidence do you have in these records that would connect them to these two wrecks?" Kinga inquired.

"There's a lot of artifacts that would survive. The ceramics would survive, the glass bottles that are very specific in this period would survive. That's what we focus on."

Alannah was itching to try and crack the mystery of the ancient cultural debris off Punta Cahuita. "Sounds like we need to go diving!"

SIN CITY

Three and a half centuries ago, Port Royal was the Las Vegas of the Americas. Pirates, cutthroats, and the meanest criminals on the planet squandered up to three thousand "pieces of eight" a night in Sin City on the island of Jamaica. Port Royal was a mecca for selling and exporting goods, making fortunes on the island's 246 sugar plantations, and partying like there was no tomorrow.

Strolling along the quays, newcomers were stunned by the hundreds of ships in harbor; markets full of fresh fish, fruit, and meat; and a hundred ways to be entertained by bear gardens, cockfighting, billiards, music houses, and "all manner of debauchery." "Vile strumpets and common prostratures" beckoned buccaneers from the entrances of alehouses. Goldsmiths, artisans, and traders worked out of two hundred buildings up to four storys high. Every drink imaginable was available in the town said to have a tavern for every ten of its 6,500 residents. Port Royal was the largest and richest English town in the Americas, rivaled only by Boston. Rents were higher than in London, wages three times greater.

Port Royal was everything Europe's rulers feared. Yet its mayhem was all authorized by royal approval. The governors of Jamaica encouraged pirates to frequent the harbor to scare off Spanish and French attacks. The Sodom of the New World grew dirty rich by raiding Spanish shipping. It became the wickedest city in the world. But it also helped create a New World culture.

All along the docks and in the taverns, a unique sight in these unjust times were Black sailors laughing and partying alongside white crews. Jamaica was a bizarre contradiction. The forty-five thousand slaves from mostly Ghana and Nigeria sweating on the sugar plantations by 1703, rising to three hundred thousand by 1800, were the cornerstone of the island's riches. And yet former African captives and escaped African slaves made up 25–30 percent of pirate crews. On the docks of Port Royal, the most unlikely of human experiments played out: equal rights for fellow man, and damn where he came from.

Next to human captives, slave ships carried gold, ivory, and untold exotic wonders. Slave ships were big investments, and the lure of their booty attracted pirate attacks. Pirates started ransacking European trade along the coast of West Africa in 1683. Their disruptive powers peaked during Queen Anne's War between France and England from 1702 to 1713. Around six hundred pirates chased glory off West Africa, taking more than one hundred slave ships.

Many of the great pirate boats started out as slavers. Blackbeard's flagship, armed with forty cannons, the *Queen Anne's Revenge*, had been a French Guinea trader from Nantes heading to Martinico called the the *Concorde*. In its hold Edward Thatch (aka Blackbeard) found 516 enchained Africans from Whydah in Benin. Black Sam Bellamy's own flagship, the *Whydah Gally*, had sold six hundred Africans and Jamaicans and was heading home to London with its payout of gold, silver, and jewels when the pirates seized it. John Bowen's *Speaker*, a former five-hundred-ton, fifty-cannon French warship, was a slave ship before he took it in Madagascar.

Pirates lived outside the law. Some ran away from slavery; others fled the fear of being forcibly press-ganged into Europe's navies. In common they refused to be treated like disposable objects. Sam Bellamy especially hated "snivelling Puppies, who allow Superiors to kick them about Deck at Pleasure." In Charles Johnson's *The History of the Pyrates* (1728), Captain Mission set out the pirates' vision from the deck of another seized slave ship:

> That no Man had Power of the Liberty of another . . . That for his own part he had not exempted his Neck from the galling Yoke of slavery, and asserted his own Liberty, in order to enslave others. That however these Men were distinguished from the Europeans by their Colour, Customs, or Religious Rites, they were the Work of the same Omnipotent Being,

and endued with equal Reason: Wherefore he desired they might be treated like Free men (for he would banish even the name of Slavery from among them).

Captain Mission was a fictitious pirate who founded the ultimate pirate democracy on the African island of Libertalia. The real Libertalia was Madagascar in eastern Africa, beyond the Cape of Good Hope, frequented by Henry Avery and Captain William Kidd and where pirates found sanctuary and married local women.

On the decks of the pirate ships of Samuel Bellamy, Edward England, Blackbeard, and Olivier La Bouche, up to one third of the crew members were Black—eighty-eight Africans among Bartholomew "Black Bart" Roberts's crew of 368, and 60 Africans in Blackbeard's crew in 1717. Blacks like Diego de Los Reyes, Ipseiodawas, John Mapoo, and Diego Grillo earned enough respect from crew members to be voted leaders of pirate ships. Abraham Samuel worked as a quartermaster, and Caesar, a former slave owned by Tobias Knight of North Carolina, was a Black officer with Blackbeard.

The counterculture born on the decks of pirate ships made them the most color-blind places in the world. Crews like on the *Whydah Gally* included English, Irish, Scottish, Welsh, French, Dutch, Spanish, Swedish, Native American, African American, and African men, all enjoying revolutionary liberty, equality, and fraternity. Black pirates had the right to bear arms, voted with the rest of the crew—one man, one vote—got an equal share of treasure and, when caught, were hanged next to their brothers in arms.

Many of the Golden Age of Piracy's big names—Henry Morgan, Calico Jack Rackham, Anne Bonny, and Mary Read—cut their teeth in Jamaica. Near the entrance to Port Royal, Rackhams Cay remembers the spot where he was hanged at Gallows Point. Calico Jack was left in a cage as a warning to would-be copycat offenders. And somewhere in its waters lies Bartholomew Roberts's pirate ship the *Ranger*, sunk in a hurricane of 1722.

It was in Jamaica, among the vice dens of Sin City, that enslaved Africa helped plant the first seeds of democracy in the Americas.

AFRICATOWN

Africatown—Near Mobile, Alabama

People were not all that was brought from Africa during the transatlantic slave trade. Their knowledge came with them. Knowledge that helped give birth to the world we live in, even though few recognize the roots of so much musical, culinary, and mathematical inspiration. The talents, traditions, and memories of the enslaved Africans helped create the culture of the New World in fresh ways that we are only now beginning to fathom.

Today, Africatown looks like many sleepy places on the western coast of Alabama. Kids play pickup basketball games in backyards behind wooden-shuttered one-story homes. Look carefully and something unusual stirs. On the approach between the town and the port city of Mobile, a mural of a ship welcomes visitors along Bay Bridge Road. The white-hulled schooner with three masts skimming over choppy blue seas is the *Clotilda*.

Africatown was started from scratch by captives forcefully trafficked on the *Clotilda*, the last illegal slave ship to arrive in America in the summer of 1860. Five years after 110 men and women were stowed in its swift hull—on the back of a bet—the end of the American Civil War set them free. Without the money or support to make their way home, they started the first purely African town in America.

In the heart of Africatown, a bronze bust proudly celebrates the tough life of Cudjo Lewis, one of its founders. Cudjo lived through times of monumental change in America, World War I, and the Great Depression. His defining challenge was being trafficked at age nineteen from his home among the Yoruba people in Benin on the *Clotilda*. Cudjo was born Kossola (Kazoola)—meaning "my children do not die any more"—in the town of Bantè in Dahomey. Kazoola was the last human to be locked into America's last slave ship and died in 1935, one of the crossing's last survivors. He had gone from being the grandson of an officer of a king in Africa, singled out to train as a "special ops" soldier, handling his town's justice and security, to being forced into the lowest state of being, slavery in America. Kazoola was the last survivor of a group of people who were born in Africa, trafficked to the New World, enslaved, liberated and experienced Jim Crow laws in the American South.

People always talk about the transatlantic slave trade as if it is ancient history. But it is living memory. Black-and-white photos of Kazoola wearing his Sunday best still exist. Piecing together the traumatic exodus of most slave ship captives, taken in tribal raids, crossing the Middle Passage, and forcibly settled in the Americas is a tall order. Few wanted to remember or knew how to write about it.

Fragments of oral memory endure for the millions sold into slavery and their descendants. The surviving stories of a few successful Africans—Olaudah Equiano, Ottobah Cugoano, and Venture Smith—can be counted on one hand. Next to nothing is known about the lives and hopes of the ordinary millions. Which makes the *Clotilda* crucial to US and world history. A tremendous amount of information came from the trials of the *Clotilda* Africans in their own words.

America's Last Slave Ship

Timothy Meaher thought he could laugh at the law all the way to the bank. Which is exactly what he did. America banned the transatlantic slave trade on January 1, 1808. Decades later, plantation owners and speculating merchants were still busting open loopholes to keep Africa's forced labor flowing.

The Meaher brothers moved to Alabama from Maine to strike it rich in Mobile, the second greatest exporter of white gold—cotton—in America after New Orleans. The city's steep profits were earned from a single moneyspinning product. As a Massachusetts journalist wrote of Mobile in the 1850s, "People live in cotton houses and ride in cotton carriages. They buy cotton, they sell cotton, think cotton, eat cotton, drink cotton, and dream cotton. They marry cotton wives, and unto them are born cotton children . . . It is the great staple—the sum and substance of Alabama."

Meaher and his brothers James and Burns had fingers in the whole supply chain: a plantation, shipyard, and steamships. Throughout the 1850s, Mobile had been the slave-trading emporium of Alabama, a slave society at the center of the South's internal slave trade. After the ban on slavery came in, the state's fields ran the risk of being emptied of muscle. Mobile needed to find cheaper workers faster. Male African slaves already working in America were selling at an all-time high of $2,400 in 1860, about $49,000 in today's money, a 100 percent hike on prices a decade earlier.

Timothy Meaher did not believe the ban on the transatlantic slave trade could hold. He put his money where his mouth was, betting "a thousand dollars that inside two years I myself can bring a shipful of n-----s right into Mobile Bay under the officers' noses." He just laughed when his friends warned he would end up hanged.

THE *CLOTILDA*

- The *Clotilda*, the Americas' last slave ship
- One-deck schooner, two masts, copper-sheathed hull, twelve-man crew
- 26.2 meters long, 7.0 meters wide, 120 tons
- Owned by William Foster
- Normally used in the timber trade
- Commissioned for the slave trade by Timothy Meaher

- Left Mobile Bay, Alabama, in March 1860, carrying $9,000 in gold to buy slaves
- Reached Whydah, Bight of Benin, May 1860
- Loaded 110 captives, returned to Mobile Bay, July 1860
- *Clotilda*'s captives founded Africatown, 1866

Meaher supposedly invested $35,000 in the *Clotilda* and commissioned William Foster, its original owner, to give it a thorough makeover. Tall masts and broad sails were added to turn the schooner into more of a racing yacht, able to outrun pirate ships and the Royal Navy. Water, rice, beef, pork, sugar, flour, bread, and eighty casks of "n----r rum" were stored in the lowest hold to feed the twelve-man crew for four months and, on the way back, up to 130 Africans, for eight weeks. The "slave food" was hidden under a cargo of timber ready to be turned into platforms, partitions, and beds for captives in Africa. Foster was handed $3,500 in trade goods and $9,000 (about $185,000 today) in gold to buy 125 Africans. The captain sailed off with false papers and the flags of various nations to hide the ship's true intentions.

Meaher no doubt read with great curiosity in the November 9, 1858, edition of the *Mobile Register* how "The King of Dahomey was driving a brisk trade in slaves, at from $50 to $60 each, at Wydah." King Ghezo of the Fon people may have had his arm twisted by British forces to sign a treaty abolishing the slave trade, but the cash brought in from local palm oil was small potatoes. Cuba's hunger for illegally trafficked Africans persuaded Ghezo to rip up the 1852 peace treaty. And so the *Clotilda* headed for Whydah in Dahomey at the heart of the Slave Coast in July 1860, anchoring offshore six weeks after leaving Alabama.

The ship's timing was lucky for the Americans. King Ghezo was shot dead while on a military campaign the year before. His son, King Glèlè (named Badohun, which meant "terror in the bush"), sacked enemy towns with his twelve-thousand-strong army to avenge his father's death. Anyone trying to flee through town gates was decapitated, their heads hanged on the belts of Fon warriors, Kazoola remembered. The rest of the captives of the massacre were "yoked by forked sticks and tied in a chain," then marched three days to Whydah near the Bight of Benin and locked up in wooden pens.

William Foster offered the "ebony prince" in charge of trade in Whydah $100 each to buy 125 people. Eight days later, permission was given. America's last cargo of illegal Africans were farmers, fishermen, and traders mostly captured by the Dahomey army. The rest were refugees and victims of kidnappings. Some worshipped Islam, others tribal Vodun, Orisha, or nothing. They came from Benin and Nigeria. All the different cultures, histories, religions, and languages were locked up in one slave pen. The strangers were as foreign to each other as the countries of Europe are today. They all spoke different tongues.

The identities of the enslaved were taken away. Their heads would have been shaved to stop outbreaks of lice at sea, a humiliating cultural violation. Africans' hair—sculpted, shaved, twisted, braided, rolled, woven, and adorned with beads, gold, silver, feathers, grass, combs, pins, seeds, and shells—were windows into identity. Hairstyles marked at a glance ethnicity, family, social status, and professions. The captives' names were taken away, too. Gumpa from the Fon tribe became Peter Lee and Kanko of the Yoruba, Lottie Dennison.

Crossing the Middle Passage took forty-five days. The captives remembered that the loud banging of the water against the *Clotilda*'s hull and thunderous wind in the sails sounded like "a thousand beasts" in the bush. The Africans felt that the ship was constantly rolling high up to the sky and then to the bottom of the ocean. Only after thirteen days in the Middle Passage were the cramped captives eventually allowed on deck to stretch their legs.

The arrival of the illegal slaves in Mobile was an open secret, a daring raid that made Alabama proud. The *Macon Daily Telegraph* told its readers how the *Clotilda* "moved 110 Africans onto a steamboat and headed up the river." A Louisiana newspaper, the *Delta*, reported on the "secret landing" behind the islands in Mississippi Sound near the lower end of Mobile Bay. A tug pulled the schooner to Twelvemile Island.

There the Africans were transferred onto the steamboat the R.B. *Taney* and taken up the Alabama River to a plantation below Mount Vernon. Eleven days later the captives were marched onto the steamer *Commodore* and taken down to where the Alabama and Tombigbee Rivers

met and where Burns Meaher had a plantation. The Africans were sepa-
rated into two long rows, men in one, women in the other. Some couples
were bought together and taken to Selma. The rest were divided between
the Meaher brothers and Foster. The slaves were then set to work.

Timothy Meaher was arrested and accused of illegal slaving. Under
oath he swore he never sailed on the *Clotilda*, which was technically correct, even if he owned the ship and was the brains behind the scheme.
Meaher was released on bail with little fuss. Judge William G. Jones was
a friend, after all, in whose honor Meaher had even named a steamer.
Meaher laughed about his adventures for years to come, just as he had
predicted. Meaher and William Foster became local heroes.

After slavery was abolished, the *Clotilda*'s slaves started saving up
enough cash to buy the land they were renting from Meaher and other
local plantation owners. The men sweated in sawmills and the railroads.
The women grew and sold vegetables in Mobile. The dream of Africatown, a haven away from white supremacy, became a reality in 1866. As
the only African nobleman and courtier, Gumpa—now Peter Lee—was
chosen to lead the new community.

How many Africans were illegally imported into America nobody can
say for sure. Figures vary wildly from fifteen thousand to one million.
The Meaher family still owns huge swathes of property around Mobile,
valued at over $25 million. They never admitted their role in America's
last transatlantic slave crossing. To many, the voyage of the *Clotilda* was
nothing more than a hoax.

Keeping Tune

In Africatown the *Clotilda*'s former slaves grew their own food and
built their own community, not in the American way but based on their
homeland traditions. The community had everything it needed; a grocery
store, a doctor, school, and entertainment. Africatown was a proud town
of twelve thousand people. Today just two thousand remain, the *Clotilda*'s
descendants scattered far and wide in the big cities.

Now the local community is reviving Africatown. If you head down to
Kazoola Eatery & Entertainment on Dauphin Street, the soul of Africa

lives on in food and music. Bare brick warehouse walls remember the area's commercial cotton past. Kazoola is a place to inspire, to remember the story of a community that endured so much.

Just as Africatown does not run from its past, Kazoola questions what we think we know about America's cultural inheritance from Africa. If you are lucky you might pick up Grammy Award–winning Rhiannon Giddens making the banjo sing in a late-night session. Most people think the banjo was an American instrument plucked on veranda porches by white hillbillies spitting tobacco. Folklore credits Joel Sweeney from Appomattox County in Virginia as its inventor in the early 1830s before he gave the first public performance and toured Europe.

Rhiannon Giddens has a very different take. She grew up seeing white people play the banjo and finding it cool, but not part of her culture. Later she came across musical recordings of Black musicians playing the same instrument. The more she dug into the banjo's background, the more she realized it had an ocean-spanning legacy. Long before the modern banjo became a metallic instrument to play bluegrass, it was an African and then an African-American instrument. The very emblem of being Black was the banjo.

It was only in the 1820s and 1830s that white folks started getting tuned into the banjo and paid a backhanded acknowledgement of its inspiration in blackface performances. For sixty years, blackface minstrel shows entertained middle-class America. Much earlier, the banjo, bluegrass music, and the do-si-do danced to it were brought to America by African captives trafficked on slave ships. Black folk music and musicians would inspire and teach the first generation of minstrel banjoists, including Sweeney, Billy Whitlock, and Dan Emmett, who made the song "Dixie" world famous.

Early travelers saw the banjo in its original setting in Africa as early as 1621, where it was "made of a great gourd, and a necke thereunto fastnd." A slave dealer named Nicholas Owen heard an instrument made of wood and played by the people of Sierra Leone in the mid–eighteenth century that sounded "like a bad fiddle . . . called a Bangelo." The "banza" or "banjer" was already the instrument of choice on slave plantations from Martinique to Virginia in the 1670s and 1680s, especially after the drum was banned by estate owners as slaves' potentially warlike call to arms.

Early America found the banjo greatly fascinating. On Sundays at "Negro Balls," "these poor creatures . . . generally meet together and amuse themselves with Dancing to the Banjo. This musical instrument (if it may be so called) is made of a Gourd something in the imitation of a Guitar, with only four strings and played with the fingers in the same manner. Some of them sing to it, which is very droll music indeed," wrote Nicholas Creswell of Maryland in 1774. To white ears, the rude African banjo grated. In Richmond, Virginia, Thomas Fairfax felt in 1799 that the banjo's "wild notes of melody seem to Correspond with the state of Civilization of the Country where this species of music originated."

Banjos and fiddles left a deeper impression on Mary Livermore, a governess on a Virginia plantation around 1847, who never forgot a Black dance and the lyrics chanted to accompany it:

> *Now all dis week will be as gay As am de Chris'mas time;*
> *We'll dance all night, a' all de day, An' make de banjo chime;*
> *Wi' 'nuff t' eat an' 'nuff t' drink, An' not a bit t' pay!*
> *So shet youah mouf as close as def*
> *An' all you n-----s, hol' youah bref,*
> *An' hear de banjo chime!*

Today the *Clotilda*'s descendants still celebrate the banjo being played in Kazoola's bar in Africatown. Rhiannon Giddens and her fellow musicians never forget this place's historical and cultural link to the last ship sent over to America. Most African Americans have no idea where their families came from," Rhiannon knows, "but musically, I know my lineage," she says. "There's more than one way to be connected to who we are as a community. It's not just blood."

Just as the banjo's African inspiration is increasingly appreciated, the truth behind America's last illegal slave voyage is now undeniable. The wreck of the *Clotilda* was finally discovered in 2019 near Twelvemile Island, just north of the Mobile Bay delta.

The ship really existed. It was no hoax. The whole world can now understand its plight.

CAHUITA'S CARPET
OF TREASURE

The Bribri teenagers were decked out in shorts, flip-flops, baseball caps, and gold earrings. Theirs, though, was a unique blend of African and Central American identity and culture. From their inland hideaway they set out to show Alannah, Kramer, and Kinga the shore where they believe their African ancestors were wrecked and waded to a new world. The ships may have sunk, but the captives found sanctuary.

In the shallows of Punta Cahuita on the east coast of Costa Rica, the Bribri youth had noticed a perplexing carpet of treasures that might shed light on where they came from. They wanted to understand how these far-flung goods got there and what they tell us about the sunken past.

"We are searching to discover how my ancestors came here. And to know where we came from," Anderson Rodriguez told the Florida dive team.

Kevin Rodriguez Brown added that "Trying to find these ships means a lot to us because we will get to know the history these people brought. And that history becomes our culture."

Salvador Van Dyke also hoped that whatever was out there in the Punta Cahuita could finally give a voice to the escaped African ancestors.

Guided by the Bribri teenagers, Diving With A Purpose started snorkeling around Cahuita Bay to get familiar with the underwater terrain. Everyone needed to swim carefully. This stretch of the southern Caribbean is protected. Cahuita National Park controls 2,732 acres of land and 55,200 acres of sea. On land, sloths blink at white-headed capuchin monkeys watched by kingfishers and toucans. Underwater, five hundred species of fish and orca whales make merry. Cahuita was the most stunning and least spoiled waters where Diving With A Purpose had chased slave ships so far. White beaches poured into the Caribbean's turquoise sea.

Alannah, Kramer, and Kinga had joined up with some of Diving With A Purpose's founding figures. In orange shorts and cap, the skipper of the *Gumbe* pulled the throttle. The *Sinac* motored alongside. It was a short commute: the dive site turned out to be just a few hundred meters offshore.

Kinga expected Cahuita to be an easy and fun dive. Gently undulating water in the warm Caribbean, mildly overcast skies, and a shallow seabed. What was not to like? The problem was that the survey area was huge and for more than three hundred years tides and storms had mixed artifacts lost over the centuries all over the reefs. What could have slipped off the Danish frigates, and not English or American ships, needed to be expertly picked apart.

Shafts of light lit up the top layer of Caribbean water like a chandelier, but even in just three meters' depth, swirling algae and silt made detecting any wreckage challenging. Kramer could not help but worry whether the hunt for the *Christianus Quintus* and *Fredericus Quartus* would turn into another *Leusden*.

"We can barely see anything down here. The visibility is so bad," Alannah told the surface team after a quick snorkel. The team persevered, flashlights in hand. Above the waves it was day. Below an eternal night enveloped the sunken secrets.

Kramer focused on making the most of what visibility existed. After the horrendous conditions of the English Channel and Suriname's Maroni River, this was still a breeze. He reminded the team of the prize. "Our job is to discover if there are any remains of two Danish slave ships left behind."

Whether the folklore was true or just a tall story, whether the *Christianus Quintus* and the *Fredericus Quartus* ever made it to these shores, depended on what wreckage Diving With A Purpose could find. The very identity of a group of young people depended on it.

The Wrong Turn

In 1709, the situation on the Danish frigates had gone from bad to worse. They left the Guinea coast in September 1709. The plan to take on supplies in Barbados before starting the final outbound leg to St. Thomas was abandoned after the *Christianus* and the *Fredericus* missed the British colony by sailing three degrees too far north. By November, provisions were dangerously low. Panic was setting in when an island was spotted. A boat from Jamaica fishing for sea turtles told the crew the island was Providence, modern Santa Catalina between Jamaica and Nicaragua.

More bad news. Providence was the base for English pirates and their Mosquito Coast Indian allies slave raiding the coasts of Costa Rica and Nicaragua, 125 miles away. The notorious pirate Henry Morgan had used Providence to raid Panama in 1670. If the present band of pirates heard about two shiploads of African slaves, the Danish crews could expect a sticky end. The ships had made landfall 300 miles from their intended destination. Lacking cash for supplies, they made do with turtle meat the Jamaicans gave them and got the heck out of these waters on February 19, 1710.

A new plan was hatched. St. Thomas was forgotten. Instead, on February 19, 1710, the captains set course for Portobelo in Panama. Strong currents and bad weather soon made a mockery of this plan, too. The frigates missed Portobelo by over five hundred miles. A Danish Court later decided that the captains schemed all along to sail to Panama and sell the Company's slaves at a higher price, pocketing the profits.

Lost among shark- and pirate-infested waters, Jamaican fishermen eventually piloted the frigates into the bay of Punta Caretto off Costa Rica. This latest unexpected stopover was no safer than Providence. British and Dutch privateers-turned-pirates, like the dreaded Henry Avery, Edward Mansfield, Edward Collier, Laurens de Graf, and Laurens Prins, had haunted these Caribbean shores rich with cacao haciendas. British masters were known to pay top dollar for African labor. They did not ask where the enslaved came from. In the year when the *Christianus* and *Fredericus* anchored off Costa Rica, cocoa exports to Europe were at an all-time high, all on the back of Black slave labor.

The Danish ships were now uncomfortably close to the lucrative cocoa estates of the Matina Valley. There, pirates and Miskito Indians raided and traded slaves. A charismatic Miskito king called Jeremy, sixty years old and six feet tall, with hair hanging down to his shoulders and a voice like a bear, was thick as thieves with British merchants. Jeremy was contracted to "hunt Negroes."

COSTA RICAN COCOA, FOOD OF THE GODS

Venezuela's cacao plantations at Caracas started declining in the mid-seventeenth century just when the West's love affair with cacao took off. New sources of chocolate included Porto Limón in Costa Rica's Matina Valley, which the local governor called "the best cacao groves ever seen." Around 140,000 cacao trees ringed the valley in the late seventeenth century. Annual crops might reach 107 tons of beans. Other haciendas flourished in the Barbilla and Reventazón Valleys. Chocolate became the region's biggest moneymaker.

Plantation owners hired Spaniards, Blacks, and mulattos at two pesos a day—more than soldiers earned—paid in cacao, clothing, or other goods. African slave numbers rose by 48 percent in the 1700s to service a mini boom in Costa Rica's cacao trade. The strongest men cleared the thick forests; the less robust watered, shaded, and weeded plants. The average farmer owned 1,900 trees.

Compared to the Americas' sugar plantations, conditions were less severe in Costa Rica. Slaves lived in their own wood and palm thatch houses and ate plantains, oranges, avocados, and sapote fruit. Africans from Guinea introduced traditional rice cultivation to the area and owned rice fields. Because cacao beans were legal tender on Costa Rica, slaves had easy access to money. Slaves also transported cacao crops to the coast of Cartago for sale to Dutch, English, and Miskito-Zambo Indigenous group.

Cacao beans exported from sixty-two ports from Mexico to Central America hooked the West. Cardinal Richelieu of France used chocolate as a drug to cure "the vapors of his spleen." It also treated infectious diseases. Cacao beans were traded into Massachusetts Bay by 1668, and chocolate almonds went on sale in French confectioners about the same time.

Italian immigrant Francesco Bianchi opened White's Cocoa House next to St. James's Palace in London in 1693. Women thought chocolate was an aphrodisiac and sipped the drink in the bedroom. By 1701 chocolate was being drunk and eaten in cakes across the West. In the 1720s England imported around 230,854 pounds of cacao beans a year. Rich and pleasurable, the eighteenth-century scientist Carl Linnaeus called cacao the food of the gods.

The Danish frigates were critically low on food supplies, and the Danes were deep in Jeremy-hunting land. The crews were rattled. They demanded the African captives be released to save the provisions and what food was left be divided among them. They also wanted a month's pay to jump ship and pay their way to safety. When the captains refused, the crews threatened mutiny.

Events were fast getting out of hand. Captain Dirk Fijfe had no option but to release the slaves of the two ships "against my better judgment." On March 4, 1710, the Africans vanished into the bush. It was too little too late. The mutiny was on. The crew smashed open the company's chests holding African gold and counted it out among themselves. To hide the crime and cover their tracks, they burnt the *Fredericus Quartus* down to the waterline. The boatswain on the *Christianus Quintus* landed the crew on the beach and cut the ship's anchor cable, leaving the frigate to break up in the surf.

A Jamaican ship took the crew to Portobelo, the captains forcefully traveling with them. Costa Rican colonists rounded up 105 of the Danish frigates' Africans and auctioned them to the local plantation owners. The rest—approximately 700 souls—were never seen again.

Officers' Wine

Searching for the remains of the Danish ships, the team snorkel-dived up and down until they were drunk with dizziness, their faces peering inches above the seabed searching for anything out of the normal. The water felt eerie, silent, and foreboding, unlike the forest so full of light, noise, and life. It was as if the divers could sense that something terrible happened in these waters.

The underwater visibility here is tricky any time of year. On exceptional days, dozens of species of fish flit across light yellow brain, elkhorn, and blue staghorn corals. Sea fans and gorgonians dance in the shallows. Ever since an earthquake in 1991, though, Cahuita's thirty-five types of coral beds have been fighting for survival.

Earthquakes had uplifted a large section of coral reef by about ten feet. At low tide it became exposed to air and sun and rapidly died. When it rains the visibility drops to a few feet as silt floods down in the Estrella River, a threat on the rise caused by the legal and illegal logging of inland forests. The stripped mountain slopes erode swiftly and end up offshore, blocking the sunlight the reefs need to survive.

Even on endlessly sunny days, the reefs are endangered. Too much fertilizer from the local banana plantations creates vast blooms of plankton that again block the sunlight and poison the water. Seven of Cahuita's thirty-four coral species have disappeared. Both reefs and old ships have been wrecked and need saving.

Alannah was for calling it a day and returning to the Robinson Crusoe beach to chill out. Just then Anderson Rodriguez whooped with delight. The divers made their way to where the top of a black glass bottle, its base snapped off, was perched on top of the reef. Kinga and Anderson high-fived underwater. This was more like it.

Kamau Sadiki, a lead instructor with Diving With A Purpose, took a good look and later told the Bribri teenagers that "What we've found here could be significant. It looks like a period bottle. This brown in color, seems like it might have some manufacturing defects on it. But, it's definitely not a modern bottle."

Did the bottle once hold wine drunk by the officers of the *Christianus Quintus* and the *Fredericus Quartus*? Did the date and style fit?

Fanning out from the bottle a carpet of finds started to appear. One discovery led to another. Half of a buff-colored ceramic plate, possibly Spanish, then an intact champagne bottle and a slice of a white dish with a blue border made in Staffordshire in England. The finds were hard to read and could date anywhere between the seventeenth and nineteenth centuries. The next find looked more promising, the lower half of a fancy, must-have stoneware jug decorated with cobalt blue flowers made in the great pottery kilns of Westerwald in the German Rhineland. All European shipping used these fancy table wares. Right time, right place.

Dr. Melody Garrett, a Diving With A Purpose instructor, was impressed. "I've never really seen so many artifacts scattered around in the same place," she told the team.

Anderson Rodriguez was buzzing. "You cannot see very well," he admitted, "but we found many pottery pieces, bottles. I'm very emotional because it's something new and I hope we can keep finding things."

Kramer agreed and felt that "Archaeologically speaking, this is a treasure trove right here. Items all over the place, so now is the time where we need to get back in and start to document and report these things."

From the one snorkel dive it was clear that, despite its remote setting, a great deal of maritime traffic visited the Punta Cahuita over the years. The big question was: Were the finds from two Danish slave ships? Were the discoveries junk, slung overboard by passing ships, or wreckage? Kinga was cautious but optimistic, telling the team that "We don't yet know whether these artifacts are from the slave ships we're trying to identify but finding so many so close together is a giant step forward."

The four small dive boats floated peacefully on a flat sea lit up by a golden sun. Costa Rica was sharing a final light show before night fell. It was time to pack up, collect thoughts, and plan the next day's dive. Would the *Christianus* and the *Fredericus* give up their jealously guarded secrets?

Reading Pottery

Andreas and Melody set themselves up in a sandwich shop, surrounded by tropical trees, to examine photos of the sunken finds scattered across Cahuita National Park on her computer. Melody was still trying to pick apart the meaning of the many artifacts recorded on the last dive. Only Andreas would be able to tell if they matched the two Danish slave ships that may have introduced enslaved Africans into Bribri culture.

"What do you think?" Melody eagerly asked about the white broken piece of ceramic plate with a blue rim border.

Andreas hardly hesitated, reading the past like most people read books. "This plate? I'm quite sure that that is after 1850. So, it's not related to the wrecks," he started out on a low.

Next Melody asked about a gray-and-blue German jug.

"Could be from the right period," Andreas mused, not sold on the date. "It could also be 150, 180 years more modern."

The photo of the jug was now changed for the broken bottle neck spotted by Anderson Rodriguez. Andreas's eyes widened. "Oh, this is an interesting bottle. It's difficult to see in this photo, but it looks like it has the shape of an onion bottle. One of the things that we know from the cargo list is that we have sixty-six bottles of La Combe Brûlée wine. And we also know that we have French brandy."

Andreas ran his finger down the cargo list for the *Christianus Quintus* and *Fredericus Quartus*, tapping the entries showing the crates of Burgundy's finest shipped for sale in the Americas.

"So, this particular piece is quite promising then," Melody checked.

"This is definitely an interesting object," he confirmed.

The finds carpeting Cahuita's shallows were promising but no slam dunk. Artifacts from so many time periods all mixed together made it impossible to be certain any came from the Danish ships. Time to change tack. Andreas decided the team needed to focus on one very specific signature object that could only have come from Denmark.

The Danish marine archaeologist shared his thoughts with Melody, Alannah, Kramer, Maria, and Kinga. "We know that there are all these different types of cargo, handguns, and there's bottles of wine and brandy. But one thing that is very specifically Danish is the yellow brick."

Hoping for something more glamorous, Kinga was at first taken aback. "The yellow brick?" she enquired.

Andreas explained that the archives showed that Danish frigates like the *Christianus* and *Fredericus* typically carried around forty thousand bricks. The thousands of Danish yellow bricks doubled up as ballast and saleable cargo to sell to the European colonies in the West Indies.

Alannah also struggled to grasp what made bricks a big deal. "What would make the bricks 'Danish'?" she checked.

"The size of Danish bricks was very specific," Andreas explained, pulling an example out of his rucksack. This was classic archaeological sleuthing. Often it is not the statement pieces, silver coins or gold bars, that catch the imagination, but the humblest everyday object.

The team handled the brick while Andreas laid out how "This is a brick found in Denmark. This size is specifically Danish. And it's very often that they're yellow. If you were to find bricks of this size and this color, then it would definitely be a smoking gun."

"There would be a lot of bricks?" Alannah asked.

"Probably not going to look like a gigantic pile of forty thousand bricks, but it will be sort of a substantial area of bricks," Andreas said without being able to go into specifics. After three hundred years being battered on the seabed, nobody could tell for sure what the brick pile would look like today.

Bricks were not what Kinga expected the case nailing the discovery of the *Christianus* and *Fredericus*, and the emotional question of Bribri origins, to hinge on. She cleared her mind and refocused. "So, this is what we're looking for. This will be our smoking gun. Ok, follow the yellow brick road," she said to the brick and smiled at her dive buddies.

SOUL FOOD

Jekyll Island, Georgia, is where the second to last slave ship made landfall in the United States. In November 1858 the *Wanderer* brought in 409 people from Angola. Like in the *Clotilda* years, the transatlantic slave trade was illegal. Little wonder its captain chose this well-hidden marsh covered with eel grass and wild rice to dock his cargo and sell the Africans across the Deep South.

Today on Jekyll Island's wild and serene beaches visitors leave their cares at the causeway and film directors check in to shoot the likes of *X-Men* and *Magic Mike*. It is also home to activist, farmer, and chef Matthew Raiford, who learned his trade in the finest international schools of cuisine. Since childhood, he always knew a different way to cook. Not the European way but what he picked up from his grandmother—and *that* was much tastier.

After a military career, and then plying and teaching his trade far and wide, Matthew returned to his family farm on Jekyll Island to celebrate African American culture through food. He learned to cook from his father, who learned from his mother. She used to pick up discarded chicken gizzards from a local slaughterhouse and spice them up with pepper and salt to fry. For Matthew, traditional home cooking—African cooking—is medicine.

He lives on the family farm on land the Raifords have owned since 1874. They are still working the soil today the old ways. Matthew cooks the Gullah Geechee way. Gullah Geechee culture is part of his heritage. It's an African tradition that took root on the Sea Islands along the Atlantic coast of Georgia, Florida, and North and South Carolina. During the

Civil War, white plantation owners fled in fear of former slaves seeking revenge. The African population that was left on its own was forced to hone its survival skills. How do you make a living with no education and are stuck on a barrier island? It was at places like Jekyll Island that much of what the world sees today as Southern cuisine was invented by enslaved and then freed Africans.

Despite being shackled and torn from everything they knew crossing the Atlantic, the culture Africans brought across the waves included their cuisine—spices, salts, and cookery methods. The exiles often carried not just memories but a piece of home with them, braiding seeds into their hair. They planted what looked like ornaments in their new destinations. Every time they ate, the exiles could remember home, preserve a piece of their identity. Gullah cuisine is made up of many ingredients brought west with Africans, including rice, sweet peas, and okra.

The bridge between food preparing and cooking in West Africa and in America survives underwater. An African grindstone turned up on the wreck of the *Fredensborg*, a Danish West India Company ship lost off Tromøy in southern Norway in 1768. Strange ceramic griddle pans and cooking pots went down on the 1622 Spanish fleet off the Florida Keys and Straits of Florida. Their shapes are identical to potting traditions in Ghana and Nigeria. Even on Spanish galleons sailing between Seville, Colombia, and Havana, slaves forced to sweat below deck in kitchen galleys kept their distinct cultural cooking preferences alive for soups and stews.

The Gullah cuisine mastered by Matthew Raiford is one of the oldest world traditions practiced in America today. From South Carolina and Georgia to Jacksonville in Florida, Gullah people from Angola working coastal plantations farmed lima beans and tomatoes, raised pigs, and cooked with oysters, turtles, and shrimp. And into African dishes they mixed peanuts, okra, rice, yams, peas, hot peppers, sorghum, and watermelon. Gullah cuisine has been kept alive and kicking by these cultural exchanges since the mid–eighteenth century. And the Africans also cultivated rice like they were back home on the Rice Coast of Liberia, Sierra Leone, Senegal, Gambia, and Guinea.

Okra and gumbo, the flagship dish of New Orleans, may be a signature dish connected with the American South, but it was made in West

Africa. Louisiana's jambalaya gets its name from *ya-ya*, the West African word for rice. The South's one-pot wonders also owe deep cultural thanks to the Gullah's *dafa*, "cook everything" culinary tradition. A large part of West African cuisine's survival was the result of women keeping the home fires burning. Emeline Jones was born into servitude around 1840 as the daughter of a slave on the estate of Colonel Benedict William Hall at Eutaw in Maryland. After being trained as a house servant, she was freed before the Civil War by Hall's daughter. Jones made her way, dreaming, to the mean streets of New York.

From working as a private chef for an insurance executive at the Club House in Long Branch, New Jersey, Jones rose to feeding Presidents Garfield, Arthur, and Cleveland at the Carlton Club, where one of her appetizer specialties was crab gumbo and okra soup. On the back of presidential stamps of approval, the White House tried to poach her. One of Emeline's greatest inspirations was introducing the fried potato chip to America from her restaurant in Moon's Lake House in Saratoga, New York.

Today, Matthew Raiford cooks homestyle, vegetarian paella with sweet potato leaves, Cherokee Purple tomatoes, and Sea Island red peas. For diners preferring a bit of bite he adds sapelo clams harvested right off Jekyll Island. These tastes and traditions, typically thought of as the food of the poor or slaves, is big business. In modern Charleston, Gullah cooking lives on in hipster dishes. Every city in the United States is competing to run the best Southern restaurant. And what are they serving? Rice, peas, and fried gizzards. Along with this adoration of soul food there is a growing realization that it is not just "Southern." It's "Made in Africa."

WHERE DO I COME FROM?

Diving With A Purpose and the young Bribri divers were resting on a narrow strip of castaway beach along the east coast of central Costa Rica. The tropical forest's green branches hung over yellow sands, perhaps the very sands where African captives escaped the *Christianus Quintus* and *Fredericus Quartus* Danish frigates in 1710.

Kramer had been chatting to the locals who had dived around Cahuita for years. Diving With A Purpose had learned that there were a few more spots in deeper waters where the kind of wreckage the team was looking for might lie, final proof of the truth behind the legend of the Danish slave ships. As well as yellow bricks, the divers were also on the lookout for larger targets like cannons, cannonballs, gold, and even ivory, objects which would have accompanied slavers arriving from Africa.

Because the team was heading farther out, snorkeling would not cut it. The team would need to dive. Everyone started suiting up, strapping their buoyancy vests to dive tanks and checking that their lead belts were strung with enough weight.

Before taking to the water, above the seabed where denser finds were thought to be hidden, Kamau Sadiki talked dive plans and safety.

"Salvador is going to be the lead youth diver," Kamau told the team. "In terms of safety, I know it's not very deep, but we've had instructors drown in ten feet of water. So be aware of how much air you have remaining in your tank. Don't take any dive for granted, okay? Your life depends on your skills, your equipment, and your attitude. Everybody *comprendé*? All right. Pool's open. Let's go."

The implication did not need spelling out. Blackouts, panic, and running out of air mostly happen in just a few feet of water. Everybody needed to stay alert and keep their minds and eyes peeled.

The divers made final adjustments. Andreas Bloch tightened the straps on his buoyancy vest and checked that his mouthpiece was clear of the tiniest of grit that could block his breathing. Alannah strapped her underwater compass to her wrist. One by one the team dropped backward over the side of the dive boat into the soothing Caribbean.

The visibility was slightly better in these depths. Very soon the team started to come across shards of pottery and a bottle cemented to the reef. Small clues that would hopefully lead to something grander.

And then the shards of hope turned into the motherlode when the team glided across a cluster of cannons—exactly what sunken ships should look like in shallow waters. All of the Danish frigates' wooden superstructure would have been ripped off by currents and pounding waves within weeks and months of the sinking. The exposed ribs would have left the crew's belongings and cargo free to dance across Cahuita Bay. Only the cannons would have been far too heavy to shift, even by hurricanes. But what ship did they come from?

"The more I saw, the more there were. So that was amazing. They're beside each other, they're across each other . . ." an intrigued Melody trailed off.

To Kramer the guns had undoubtedly been underwater for an age. "There are some cannons that just look like coral. They were so heavily encrusted, the ocean's taken them back," he told the team.

Kamau focused on the technicalities. "We know distinctively that they are cannons," he pointed out. "You can see the bore on some of them, some are covered up. Cannons can give us a lot of information. We saw about eight, ten, maybe twelve. But if there's more, it could tell us the size of the vessel. We know the size of the *Fredericus* and the *Christianus*. So that would be very insightful."

And there was more wreckage to come. Even with three hundred years of coral growth covering it, there was no mistaking the shape of the team's next hit, an intact iron anchor.

"The shape of the anchor, it's about three to four meters," Kamau later told the surface support team, perched on the edge of an inflatable boat. "Comes from a very large ship just based on the size. Two flukes are there. Each one is about a foot wide, and maybe another foot and a half long. So, in beautiful shape. That's some incredible stuff. Some more evidence that we can put in the mix and try to figure out what's going on at this site."

For the teenager Bribri diver Sangye Brenes, the discovery was more than a lump of history, hopefully Danish history. "The first time I saw the anchor, for me is amazing," he shared. "I asked my grandfather and my grandmother, they both say yes, I have African ancestors. And they both had, like, connecting histories with slaves. To know that makes me feel more connected to my history."

The human rights activist Maria Suárez Toro felt that diving with a personal purpose was the best way for the local kids to make sense of who they were. "It's not in the history books. It's not in the documents," she emphasized. "And if they find it themselves, they begin asking the right questions. And the right question is, where do I come from? What has that meant in the life of me and my community?"

The pieces of the puzzle were falling into place. But those elusive bricks that would slam-dunk the ship's identity were still missing in action. The team needed to hunt down the start of the yellow brick road.

ROOTS, ROCK, REGGAE

S omething in the air—or water—lit the touchpaper of rebellion in Jamaica. The island was not just a hotbed of pirates and smuggling. Its sugar plantation slaves had an exceptionally violent and organized culture of resistance. Britain's largest island in the Caribbean saw a revolt almost every decade for 180 years. Is it any coincidence that reggae's musical fight for freedom took flight in Jamaica?

West Africa's dazzling music and dance echoed across the Middle Passage to the Americas on the back of slave ships, where captives were forced to sing and dance for exercise and distraction. Britain's first Black political activist, the writer Olaudah Equiano, trafficked out of the Kingdom of Benin in 1756, remembered his home tribe the Igbo as "a nation of dancers, musicians, and poets."

Beyond the need to "dance the slaves" to keep them fit for market, some ships' captains encouraged singing and music to keep the Africans' spirits up. Controlling morale dampened revolt, they hoped. Crews kept instruments—tambourines, fiddles, and bagpipes—while on some crossings music was improvised by captives thumping upturned copper soup and stew kettles. The exiles sung sorrowful tunes about their wretched condition and put their ill-fated experiences to music. As "The Sorrows of Yamba; Or, the Negro Woman's Lamentation" sang around 1790:

> At the savage Captains beck;
> Now like Brutes they make us prance:
> Smack the Cat about the Deck,
> And in scorn they bid us dance.

A nineteenth-century slave smuggler also remembered how

> Our blacks were a good-natured lot and jumped to the lash
> so promptly that there was not much occasion for scoring
> their naked flanks. We had tambourines aboard, which
> some of the younger darkies fought for regularly, and every
> evening we enjoyed the novelty of African war songs and
> ring dances, fore and aft, with the satisfaction of knowing
> that these pleasant exercises were keeping our stock in good
> condition and, of course, enhancing our prospects of making
> a profitable voyage.

Elsewhere, the "entertainment" was more like idle sport to distract
bored crews. The surgeon on the Brazilian slaver the *Georgia* described
how a week off Calabar in 1827, "I found that the captain and crew were
desperadoes of the worst kind . . . the ship became half bedlam and half
brothel. Ruiz, our captain, and his two mates set an example of reckless
wickedness. They stripped themselves and danced with black wenches
while our crazy mulatto cook played the fiddle. There was little attempt
at discipline and rum and lewdness reigned supreme."

Slavery in the Americas may have broken African bodies, but it never
destroyed the fierce African spirit. Jamaica's wild, forested countryside,
tall, rugged mountains, and hidden valleys made an ideal setting for guer-
rilla warfare by runaway slaves. The combination of a never-ending fear
of food shortage, foreign invasion, five communities of trouble-making
Maroons that escaped since 1655, and the high slave death rate made
Jamaica a powder keg.

With its three hundred thousand slaves by 1800, most trafficked from
Ghana, followed by Dahomey, the island's slave communities had little
fear about rising up against their British masters when anger bubbled
over into rage. In 1673, for instance, two hundred slaves on Major Selby's
plantation in St. Ann's, almost all Coromantee from Ghana, killed their
master and thirteen whites, then plundered nearby estates. Jamaica's
forest fire of rebellious slaves still burned bright in 1730 when Governor
Robert Hunter reported that "The Slaves in rebellion, from the increase
of their numbers by the late desertions from several settlements . . . are

grown to that height of insolence that your frontiers, that are no longer in any sort of security, must be deserted."

Maroon villages by 1736 had grown into the three rebel towns of St. George's, St. Elizabeth, and St. James, the largest inhabited by a thousand runaways. Africa had won. On March 1, 1739, the Leeward Maroon rebels signed a peace treaty that gave them freedom, the right to own land, hunt hogs, sell goods at market, and seek justice through magistrates if any whites violated the peace terms.

JAMAICA'S SLAVE PEACE TREATY

Articles of Pacification with the Maroons of Trelawney Town, Jamaica, Concluded March the first, 1738:

"First, That all hostilities shall cease on both sides for ever . . . Secondly, That the said Captain Cudjoe, the rest of his captains, adherents, and men shall [live] for ever hereafter in a perfect state of freedom and liberty . . . Thirdly, That they shall enjoy and possess, for themselves and posterity for ever, all the lands situate and lying between Trelawney Town and the Cockpits, to the amount of fifteen hundred acres . . . Fourthly, That they shall haven liberty to plant the said lands with coffee, cocoa, ginger, tobacco, and cotton, and to breed cattle, hogs, goats, or any other flock, and dispose of the produce or increase of the said commodities to the inhabitants of this island; provided always, that when they bring the said commodities to market, they shall apply first to the customs, or any other magistrate of the respective parishes where they expose their goods to sale, for a license to vend the same."

Across the Gulf, on American soil, the African exiles kept their musical traditions alive, too. Just as sea captains encouraged singing and dancing to keep up morale, plantation owners allowed dances to give their workers something to look forward to. As well as the banjo, the fiddle commonly described in early slave dances was not the European violin, but an African gourd fiddle made to an African design. Isaac D. Williams, a former slave, described how:

> We generally made our own banjos and fiddles, and I had a fiddle that was manufactured out of a gourd, with horse hair strings and a bow made out of the same material. When we made a banjo we would first of all catch what we called a ground hog, known in the north as a woodchuck. After tanning his hide, it would be stretched over a piece of timber fashioned like a cheese box, and you couldn't tell the difference in sound between that homely affair and a handsome store bought one.

Music brought a rare breath of fresh air for the enslaved to stay connected to their African heritage and, at the same time, protest against their bleak conditions. Sometimes slave masters took instruments away as too noisy, foreign, or subversive. When Africans found a way to use drums to send coded beats to stage revolts, the likes of the 1740 South Carolina Slave Code banned captives from "using and keeping drums, horns or other loud instruments." No matter. Slaves started using whatever form of rhythm-making could be adapted from household spoons and washboards to "slapping juba"—using their bodies as makeshift drums. The enslaved adapted vocal rhythms in an early form of beatbox.

In dance and song African communities rebelled, mocking their masters' ways without them realizing. The Cakewalk was a subversive in-joke against white control. The humorous dance imitated English slave masters' trendy Regency moves of small skips and hops in the formal Jane Austen style. Africans found stiff dancing ridiculous compared to their own free form of expression. Whoever danced most like the whites won a cake. White masters and visitors to big house dances totally missed the point of the act, and instead were delighted that the slaves were picking up "civilized" ways. The joke—the rebellion—was on them and still is in the modern phrase "to take the cake," or to call something "a cakewalk." It was the simplicity of mocking masters that was easy.

African Americans have been setting trends ever since. Everything from bluegrass and jazz to rock 'n' roll, country, folk, and hip-hop owes a debt of inspiration to traditional African music and the culture African slaves took to America.

One musical form that Christian slave owners approved of was the African American spiritual, whose purity they were sure praised the Lord. Its essence, though, was all about the longing to free the spirit and body, safety from harm and evil, and relief from the ills of slavery. Songs like "Sometimes I Feel Like a Motherless Child" and "I'm Troubled in Mind" released despair. Other spirituals subtly lashed slavery, using biblical metaphors to protest against Black peoples' conditions, most famously the lyrics of "Go Down, Moses": *Tell ol' Pharaoh, Let my people go.* From 1871, the Fisk Jubilee Singers' tour of America and Europe introduced "Negro spirituals" to white audiences for the first time.

Toward the late nineteenth century, African American musicians fused ragtime, sacred music, and the blues to improvise jazz. The trumpeter and singer Louis Armstrong earned international recognition with his "West End Blues" in the 1920s. America's classical music was born. Ragtime may have become the United States' first popular music in 1899 after Scott Joplin's "Maple Leaf Rag" sold over a million sheet-music copies, but it was already being played in the 1870s when Black musicians spoke of "ragging a tune."

From ragtime came the blues by way of slavery in the South, whose full force was felt after the Civil War when African Americans vented their disillusionment with their treatment. Into the twentieth century the blues turned into a country style with a solo singer playing an acoustic guitar from farms to honky-tonk gin joints at the dawn of the industrial age.

W. C. Handy put the style on America's map thanks to his "Memphis Blues" in 1912 and the "St. Louis Blues" two years later. Blues became a worldwide sensation in the 1920s, reaching new heights in the soulful, haunting beauty of Ma Rainey and Bessie Smith's voices. In 1940s Chicago, the likes of Muddy Waters added gritty electric sounds and amplification, electric guitars, harmonicas, drums, bass, and piano. The Rolling Stones, Led Zeppelin, and the Beatles all credited Chicago bluesmen as their musical fathers.

Even hip-hop has a direct thread to Africa through its rapid wordplay, complex rhyming, and storytelling. Through hip-hop, African Americans found a voice in a culture of oppression. Like their ancestors' rebellion, Black rappers put the spotlight on their communities' inner-city hardships, discontent, and politics.

Rap, the most influential form of hip-hop, combines African American blues, jazz, and soul with Caribbean calypso, dub, and dance-hall reggae. Battling even comes from the African American tradition of "toasting," boastful storytelling, often political and aggressive. Today rappers use African-inspired music to tell tragic tales of decaying projects, vicious murders, and police brutality.

Groups like Public Enemy turned their people's alienation into an art, releasing albums the public could not ignore, like *It Takes a Nation of Millions to Hold Us Back*. Most of all, rap lyrics attack economic and political inequality, waging a full-scale assault on institutions that keep African Americans in poverty. Hip-hop lives at the cutting edge of cultural innovation.

Back in the Caribbean, Jamaica gave birth to perhaps the most iconic African American musical style. Reggae's rawness spoke of a time when Africa existed for its own pleasure, a continent rich with resources, traditions, science, art, and people free from the shackles of European greed. From Harlem in the 1920s, Marcus Mosiah Garvey preached "redemption through repatriation" to Blacks and, later, Rastafarians who looked back to the homeland, Africa.

Reggae's message of empowerment and struggle for social change was powerfully captured by Bob Marley's 1973 hit "Get Up, Stand Up." And artists like Papa Levi and his "Mi God, Mi King" remembered everything that came before and set the scene for reggae to become Jamaica's biggest export:

> *They tek wey we gold, jah man, them tek we silver*
> *them hang me pupa and rape me madda*
> *the ship me from the wonderful land of africa*
> *Fi slave fi dih plantation owner*
> *They take wey we name, jah man, them call we n---a*
> *the only word we know "I isa coming, massa!"*

From the early drum players on slavers crossing the Middle Passage to plantation banjo players, Black minstrel shows, and beyond, Africans in the New World have always stood proudly at the cutting edge of popular music. Every single person on planet Earth is now familiar with music influenced by slave songs and dance that came over on the likes of the *Christianus Quintus* and *Fredericus Quartus*.

THE YELLOW BRICK ROAD

On the shores of Cahuita National Park the dive team got ready for a final push. Dive tanks were lined up against railings, soldiers ready to battle for the truth of these seas' sunken past. Diving With A Purpose and their Bribri friends weaved between small blue and yellow fishing boats pulled onto the beach. They threw their gear into three dive boats, the *Aqualord*, the *Costa*, and the *Gumbe*, and headed into the bay's deeper reaches.

The cannons and the anchor were important clues, but to identify the Danish ships once and for all meant finding yellow bricks. Loads of them. Diving With A Purpose now had an emotional opportunity to search seas and minds with the Bribri youngsters and help them make sense of their roots.

The cultural debris scattered three hundred meters offshore covered a daunting search area. The location of the guns and anchor half a cannon's fire offshore gave the team hope that they were on the right track. Looking at the nearby shore, the thought that captive Africans could have made it to land made perfect sense geographically. Those bricks had to be hiding somewhere out there. Andreas waited topside anxiously while the rest of the team dived.

It did not take long for Kevin Rodriguez Brown's eagle eyes to spot a line of rectangular objects flush with the seabed, just peering above the seagrass and shifting sands. He was sure they were bricks. Kevin surfaced excitedly and shared the promising news with Andreas.

The marine archaeologist slung his dive tank over his head and dropped overboard to explore the discovery for himself. A few hand fans over the silt and what looked like a paved road appeared. Only it was a yellow brick road, the building blocks stacked on their sides by the hundreds. Andreas pulled out his measuring tape and started checking the bricks' dimensions, his fingers crossed.

Dried down on shore, Kinga shared how well the yellow brick road had hid its secrets. "At first glance, it was hard to notice that there was anything different about this spot at all," she shrugged. "But when we looked closer, there was a strange pattern. In that moment, you realize that this cold case that has been lying on the bottom of the ocean for hundreds of years is now right in front of you, about to be solved. To see that, to be in that moment, that's a historical moment."

"This hill of seabed is actually a huge pile of bricks," Kinga realized. "According to the ship's manifest, there should be forty thousand of them down here."

A description of a brick cargo on a slave trader heading to West Africa in a nineteenth-century issue of *Harper's Weekly* reported how bricks were stored on the ship's lowest level. On top were added water casks, both empty and full of rum. Next was stowed a layer of slave food, especially rice and beans, followed by the general trade cargo like cotton, flannel, muskets, and knives. Perhaps the *Christianus Quintus* and *Fredericus Quartus* bricks were loaded in much the same way.

Andreas had managed to get permission from the marine park authorities to bring up one of the bricks for testing. It was the opposite of gold and did not glitter but shone with historical promise under the Caribbean sun. Sometimes the simplest of finds turn out to be archaeological gold.

The Bribri youth high-fived in the water, hollered, and smiled. Their mission had been accomplished. Lab tests later confirmed Andreas Bloch's scientific hunch and what generations of elders had taught the Bribri. The recovered brick measured 21 x 11 centimeters, closely resembling the Danish *flensburger* brick style.

COMPUTING—OUT OF AFRICA

Africa's contribution to art, music, and dance is well-known. Less familiar is Africa's contribution to medicine, agriculture, and science. For example, fractal geometry, the mathematics of which are one of the most important tools for modeling in biology, geology, natural sciences, and information technology. Fractals is the name for patterns that repeat themselves at many different scales. They appear in rawest form in nature: trees are branches of branches, mountains are peaks of peaks, and clouds are puffs of puffs. All use self-organizing processes in their constructions, such as clusters of cells forming clusters of clusters.

Fractals exist in nature in everything from Romanesco broccoli and ferns to snowflakes, the human lungs, and DNA. They combine a maximum surface area with a maximum flow, so trees take in more light, lungs exchange more oxygen, kidneys filter more waste, neurons connect with more neurons.

Fractal geometry was only "invented" in the West in the 1970s, but mathematician Ron Eglash realized that its nature was known in Indigenous Africa over seven hundred years earlier. Looking at aerial photos of traditional villages he noticed how the Kotoko people of Cameroon built huge rectangular building complexes by adding rectangular enclosures to preexisting rectangles in acts of self-similar scaling. The people of Logone-Birni in Cameroon and villages in Zambia made their settlements from rings of rings. Ethiopian crosses found in the architecture of eight-hundred-year-old churches in Lalibela, the traditional Fulani wedding blanket, and the board game *Owari* in Ghana all share identical fractal structures.

Bamana sand divination, found universally across Africa from East to West, is the most complex example of an algorithmic approach to fractals. It is based on a binary code known in the Western world since Hugo of Santalla brought it into Spain in the twelfth century. From there it was picked up by the alchemy community as geomancy (divination through the earth). Later Gottfried Leibniz, the German mathematician, described geomancy in his book *De Arte Combinatoria* in 1666.

Moving on in time, the binary code was turned into Boolean algebra,
which ended up making possible the invention of the digital computer
and Google's self-organizing properties of the Web. In today's 24/7
world, every digital computer started life in Africa's robust algorithms
rooted in Indigenous knowledge.

The shallows of Cahuita turned out to be the hiding place of two
lost wrecks. A cluster of thirteen iron cannon and two anchors, one over
three meters long, was scattered 32–250 meters from shore down to a
depth of five meters. The brick pile, a kilometer away, proved to be the
heart of one sunken ship spanning 19 x 9.5 meters with two iron cannons, an anchor, and three millstones for grinding flour in 9–18 meters
depth. The bricks were stacked two meters high. Underneath, preserved
for centuries, must lie the wooden hull.

Old turtle traders, divers, and tourists had been plucking parts of the
wrecks out of Punta Cahuita since 1828 when a local called "Old Smith"
was convinced the two wrecks were a French and Spanish pirate ship.
Salvaged glass bottles were sold to a Panamanian antiquities collector.
Other salvaged finds included copper manilla bracelets, cannonballs,
swords, a drinking glass, glass bottles, a barrel, and a pewter tea kettle.
Tons more artifacts are no doubt preserved under the sands and river silt.

Kramer summed up what the discovery of two old slavers meant to
the Bribri divers. "Now they have an opportunity to rediscover their ties
to their past. Rediscover their contact or the connection to the enslaved
Africans who were here."

Alannah agreed. "This is about Cahuita. This is about the people
of Cahuita. This is about the Bribri. This is about the people who are
here, to find out the truth about exactly who they are as a people. And
where they came from, and how Africans were very much a part of
creating this community."

The history books record just how badly the loss of the *Christianus
Quintus* and *Fredericus Quartus* hit Denmark. After the loss, the Danish
West Indies Guinea Company lost interest in risking big investments in
dangerous voyages. From Costa Rica the ships' captains somehow made

their way back home. Anders Pedersen Waerøe survived accusations of deliberately trying to profit from the misadventure by ignoring the terms of the contract to sail to the island of St. Thomas.

His reward? Eighteen years later, from 1728 to 1735, he became governor of the Danish Gold Coast. Waerøe did not change his dubious ways, though. The captain ended up charged with illegal trade and selling African women for sexual abuse in his dungeon at Fort Christiansborg.

Down the years, between 1702 and 1730, the Danish West Indies Guinea Company lost eight of its twenty slave ships, wrecked everywhere from Norway to the Gulf of Guinea and Costa Rica. Eventually, the merchants shut up shop. A meeting of company stockholders in 1734 decided that the trade was "bad business." They voted against continuing slaving. This did not mark the end of Denmark's trafficking of African captives, just a new phase when the industry's gates were thrown open to private entrepreneurs.

By the time the trade was abolished, Danish hulls had shipped 111,040 African souls into the Americas, separating them from their homes and families. Despite cruelty and pain, their spirits endured. Over three hundred years after the sinking of the *Christianus Quintus* and the *Fredericus Quartus*, some of their descendants dove and found their history on the ocean floor off Costa Rica.